IMAGES
of America

THE PORT OF
LOS ANGELES

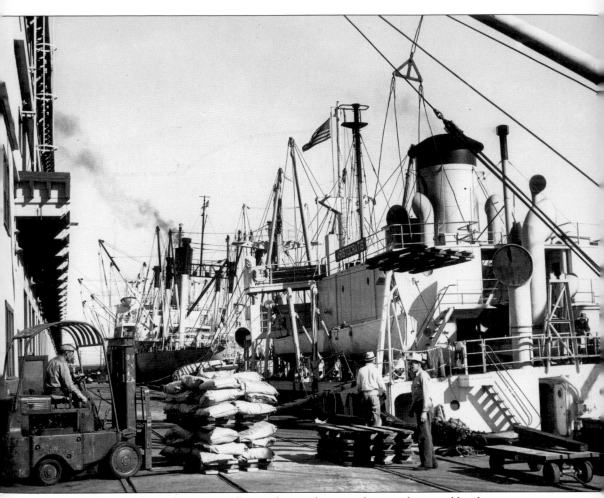

ON THE COVER: Over the years, millions of tons of cargo—from sardines and lumber to computer components and circus animals—have moved across the docks at the Port of Los Angeles. This image of the Greek-flag *Aristocratis*, a Liberty-type freighter loading bagged potash at the port in the late 1940s, evokes earlier days before containerization revolutionized global logistics forever. (Author's collection.)

IMAGES
of America

THE PORT OF
LOS ANGELES

Michael D. White

ARCADIA
PUBLISHING

Published by Arcadia Publishing
Charleston SC, Chicago IL, Portsmouth NH, San Francisco CA

Printed in the United States of America

Library of Congress Catalog Card Number: 2007935827

For all general information contact Arcadia Publishing at:
Telephone 843-853-2070
Fax 843-853-0044
E-mail sales@arcadiapublishing.com
For customer service and orders:
Toll-Free 1-888-313-2665

Visit us on the Internet at www.arcadiapublishing.com

CONTENTS

Acknowledgments   6

Introduction   7

1.   The Amazing Mr. Banning   9

2.   The Great "Free Harbor" Fight   19

3.   Lumber, Oranges, and Steel Ships   27

4.   The Postwar Boom   81

5.   The Port and the Magic Box   99

Bibliography   126

Index   127

ACKNOWLEDGMENTS

Many people had a hand in helping make this work a reality and have my heartfelt thanks for their assistance. While it's impossible to thank everyone who generously offered their help, I want to single out the reference staffs of the Burbank Public Library, the Glendale Public Library, the Pasadena Public Library, the Los Angeles Public Library, and the staff of the graphics department at Azusa Pacific University for special thanks.

I especially want to extend my sincere appreciation to the following individuals for their patience, generosity, and help in providing access to photographs, printed materials, and, above all, expert advice for this book: Julia Nagano and Jim Holdaway of the Port of Los Angeles, San Pedro, California; Dr. William O. Hendricks and Jill Thrasher of the Sherman Library in Corona del Mar, California; Tim Thomas of the Monterey Maritime and History Museum, Monterey, California; Jeff Hull and Gabrielle Pratto of the Matson Navigation Company, San Francisco, California; Dace Taube of the University of Southern California, Los Angeles, California; John Lockwood and Jason Dailey of Todd Pacific, Seattle, Washington; Don Norton and Greg Peters of the Pacific Harbor Line, Wilmington, California; Bill Dahlquist of the Los Angeles Fire Department Museum, Los Angeles, California; Melissa Lew of the Newport Harbor Nautical Museum, Newport Beach, California; and Doug Cole of NYK Line, Secaucus, New Jersey.

My heartfelt thanks also go to Jerry Roberts, Scott Davis, and Ariel Richardson of Arcadia Publishing and to everyone in my family, particularly my wife, Pam, for their patience and understanding during the course of this project.

INTRODUCTION

Standing in the shadow of Warehouse No. 1 at the mouth of the port's Main Channel, it would be very easy to conclude that the Port of Los Angeles, after all, really isn't that busy.

The occasional massive ship slowly glides up the waterway heading for her berth, the only sounds are the screeches of the gulls, the tooting of the attendant tugs, and the low, rhythmic hum of its diesel engines. In the distance, container cranes function, towering over their charges like giant birds feeding their young as, every now and then, a fuel barge or sailboat quietly, almost leisurely, passes.

The mania that many associate with both success and the operations at other ports is uniformly absent, because the Port of Los Angeles is like no other port in the world.

The sailing ships and lumber schooners that once tentatively connected the backwater mudflats of San Pedro with a much simpler world have, over the decades, given way to the giant car carriers, tankers, bulk carriers, and containerships that have turned the port into a revolving door for two-way trade moving between Southern California, the United States, and the entire world.

Like Southern California itself, the port sprawls, covering more than 7,500 acres with 270 berths along 43 miles of waterfront.

Once so shallow that visiting ships had to anchor in the harbor to have their cargo lightered to shore, the port is now the busiest container port in the entire United States and the eighth busiest in the world, handling millions of tons annually of import and export cargo, from furniture and auto parts to computer components and apparel.

During one 21st-century year, more than 2,700 ships visited the port's 27 specialized terminals, carrying containers filled with 182 million metric tons of dry and liquid bulk as well as "break-bulk" cargoes from more than 100 countries valued at more than $205 billion. More than a quarter-million imported automobiles and trucks were processed through the port's auto facility, and 1.2 million passengers crossed the gangways of the World Cruise Center.

Staggering statistics, these, but they are not the only storytelling points of any port, particularly the Port of Los Angeles. It's a story written for future generations by the countless people who, from the beginning to today, invested themselves in developing the Port of Los Angeles into what it is today—pioneer entrepreneurs such as Phineas Banning and Augustus Timms, hard-fighting visionaries like Stephen White, dedicated guardians like Frank Higbee, and dynamic leaders like Geraldine Knatz.

But it's also the story of the sailors, the immigrant fishermen, the railroad workers, the longshoremen, the artisans and craftsmen, the engineers, the common laborers, and the countless, nameless others who, literally, put the Port of Los Angeles on the world map.

The story is theirs and this book is for them.

One

THE AMAZING MR. BANNING

For generations, the economy of the Spanish imperial backwater that was Southern California centered around the Mission San Gabriel, about 40 miles inland, and the ubiquitous cattle herds that covered the landscape providing the tallow and hides—known as California greenbacks—that formed the life's blood of the region's trade activity.

In 1821, Spain ceded California to Mexico, and over the coming three decades, the hide and tallow trade flourished with regular visits by Yankee sailing ships to a lone hide house on the cliffs overlooking what is now the port's Main Channel.

Priced at $2 each, the stinking hides were processed and stacked into the ships' fetid holds and carried back around Cape Horn to tanneries in New England, where they were transformed into boots, belts, shoes, and animal harnesses.

In a story with a full cast of memorable characters, perhaps the most intriguing and compelling is Phineas Banning, the transplanted New Englander who arrived in San Pedro in 1851 at the age of 19, whose entrepreneurial vision and drive would later earn him the title "Father of Los Angeles Harbor."

Over the following 35 years, the hulking, largely self-educated Banning exercised a keen nose for business by spawning a series of ventures that would not only expand his own entrepreneurial horizons but also lay the foundation for the development of the harbor into a truly world-class port.

Banning's first venture was a local passenger and freight hauling network that eventually linked his wharf with points in five Western states.

California state senator Phineas Banning introduced the first railroad bill in Sacramento in 1867 and later lobbied to have the U.S. Congress fund the first dredging of the harbor's Main Channel and the construction of its first breakwater.

In 1869, the transplanted Yankee oversaw the construction of a rail line linking the harbor at San Pedro and the burgeoning town of Los Angeles—a 21-mile stretch of track comprising the first railroad in Southern California.

In 1885, the year Banning died, the port moved more than 50,000 tons of lumber, coal, manufactured goods, agricultural products, and other goods across the wharves he was largely responsible for building.

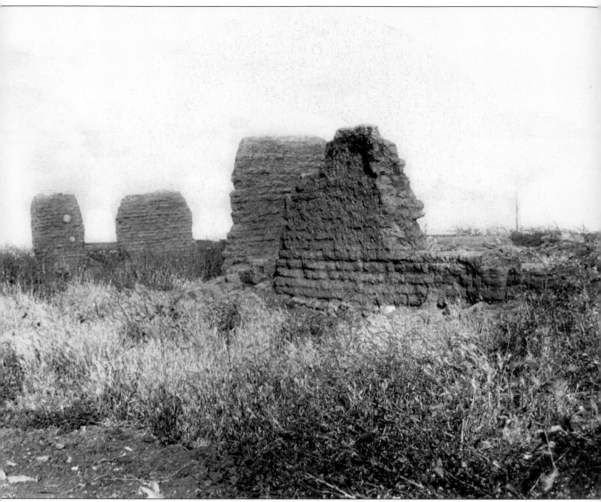

HIDE HOUSE, 1823. San Pedro's first warehouse was built on what is now the parade ground of Fort MacArthur on the bluff overlooking the harbor's Main Channel. By the end of the 1800s, all that remained of the structure were the weed-choked ruins seen in this image taken some 70 years after it was built. (Courtesy of the Title Insurance and Trust Collection, University of Southern California.)

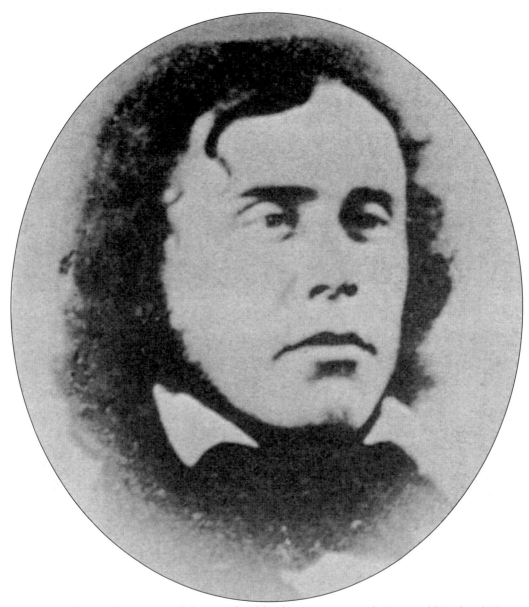

RICHARD HENRY DANA, 1835. In poor health, the inexperienced 19-year-old Richard Henry Dana dropped out of Harvard University and signed on to serve as a common seaman aboard the Yankee brig *Pilgrim*. The ship, owned by the Boston shipping firm of Bryant and Sturgis, sailed for California via Cape Horn to San Pedro, where the ship would load cattle hides and tallow for the return trip to New England. The crew of the *Pilgrim* was tasked with hauling the reeking cargo by hand from the hide house on the bluff overlooking the harbor down to small boats, which were then rowed out to the waiting brig. Dana chronicled the voyage and his labors in his classic book *Two Years Before the Mast* and was not altogether thrilled with his visit to what he called the "hell" of Southern California. (Author's collection.)

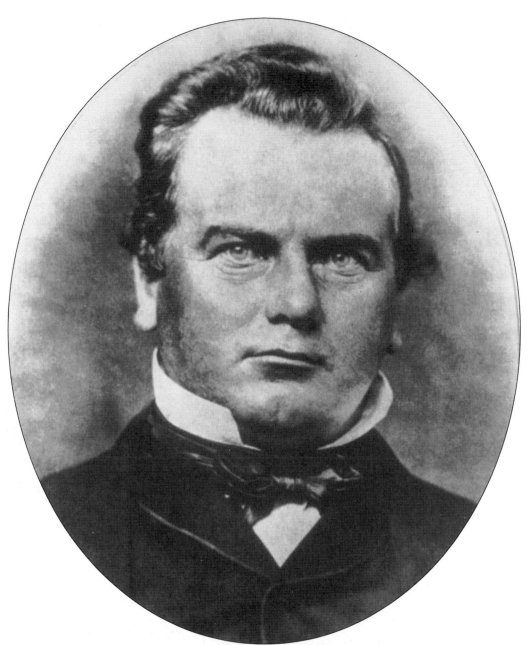

PHINEAS BANNING, 1852. Considered by many to this day to be the "Father of the Port of Los Angeles," Phineas Banning was a hard-driving Delaware-born entrepreneur who played a pivotal role in establishing San Pedro as a viable business center and transportation hub. Banning operated one of the first freighting companies at the harbor, with cargo-laden wagons linking his wharf with distant Los Angeles and points beyond. A strong supporter of the Union during the Civil War, he later served in the California state senate, playing a key role in establishing an effective transportation network to serve the greater Los Angeles region. Banning died tragically in 1885 of injuries suffered when he fell from a cable car during a business trip to San Francisco. (Courtesy of the Port of Los Angeles Archive.)

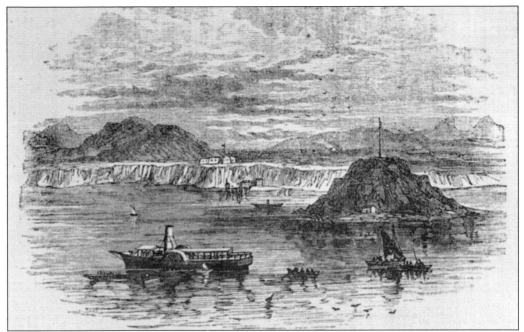

DEADMAN'S ISLAND, 1854. This rock pile was named after eight U.S. Marines were buried on the island following the Battle of Rancho Dominguez, a daylong skirmish fought between U.S. forces and local Mexicans in 1846. The island was located at what is now the extreme seaward tip of Terminal Island. (Courtesy of the Port of Los Angeles Archive.)

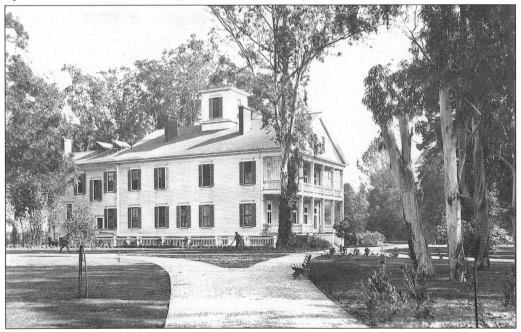

BANNING MANSION, 1864. Port pioneer Phineas Banning built his palatial home in Wilmington, which he founded in 1857 adjacent to San Pedro and named in honor of the capital of his home state of Delaware. The residence has been preserved as a museum and is now open to the public. (Courtesy of the Sherman Library.)

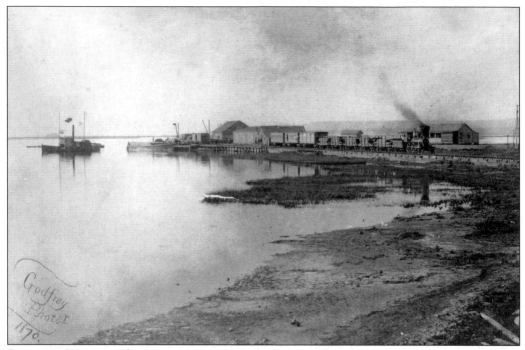

BANNING WHARF. The water at Banning's dock wasn't deep enough to permit sailing ships and steamers to tie up alongside, so he constructed large, shallow-draft lighters to move cargo of all kinds between ships anchored in the harbor and the wharf. (Courtesy of the Port of Los Angeles Archive.)

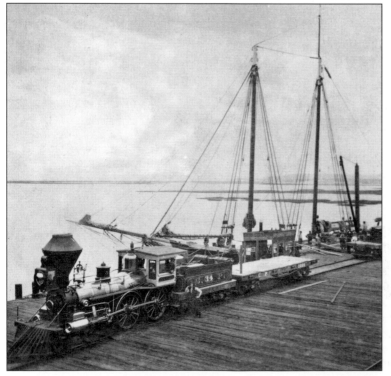

RAIL CONNECTIONS, 1870. Los Angeles and San Pedro Railway locomotive No. 34 pulls a flatcar along the tracks of the Banning Wharf as a two-masted schooner unloads its cargo of lumber. Banning started the rail service linking his wharf with distant Los Angeles in 1869. (Courtesy of the Title Insurance and Trust Collection, University of Southern California.)

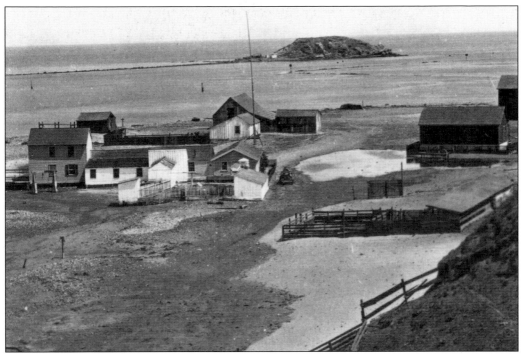

TIMMS POINT, 1870. German immigrant Augustus Timms was Phineas Banning's archrival in the efforts to develop the harbor. He built his warehouse in 1850 near what is now the Ports O' Call Village at Berths 74–77. By 1881, the warehouse had been converted into a school with 15 pupils from 14 local families attending. Timms died in 1883. (Courtesy of the Title Insurance and Trust Collection, University of Southern California.)

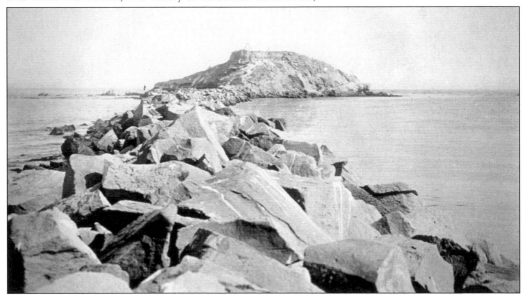

DEADMAN'S ISLAND JETTY, 1871. The harbor's first breakwater was built when a 6,700-foot-long stone jetty was constructed between Rattlesnake Island and Deadman's Island. At the same time, the harbor's main channel was deepened to 10 feet at a cost of $200,000 to reduce the amount of silt preventing ships from entering the harbor. (Courtesy of the Port of Los Angeles Archive.)

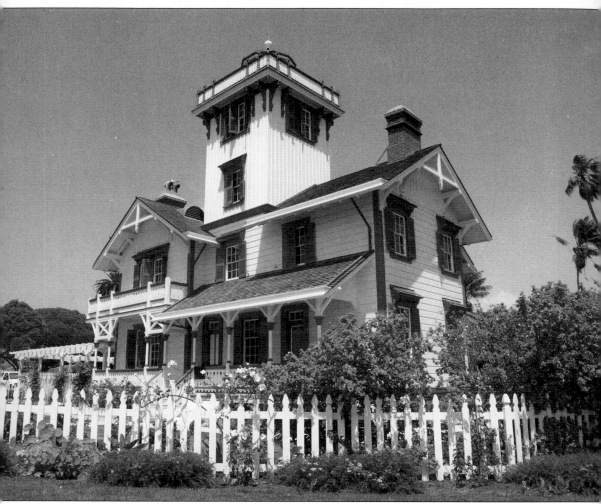

POINT FERMIN LIGHTHOUSE, 1874. Built on the highest bluff overlooking San Pedro's main channel, the Point Fermin Lighthouse was in service until World War II, when it doused its light for security reasons. The lighthouse was decommissioned after the war as radar took over the job of safely guiding ships into the harbor. (Courtesy of the Port of Los Angeles Archive.)

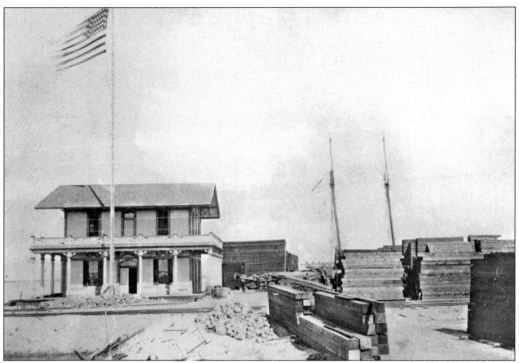

U.S. CUSTOMHOUSE, 1883. The federal government opened the harbor's first customhouse in June 1883. The building, staffed by a trio of overworked customs inspectors, was a two-story, colonnaded structure adjacent to the lumber wharf operated by the W. H. Perry Lumber Mill Company. (Courtesy of the Title Insurance and Trust Collection, University of Southern California.)

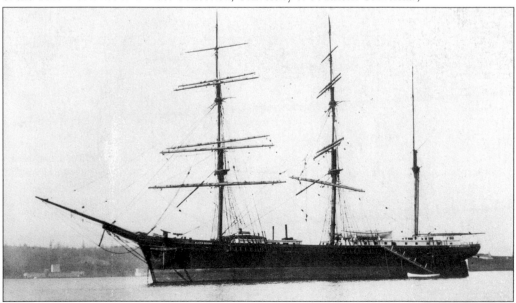

BARK ALDEN BESSE, 1889. A frequent visitor to San Pedro was the beautiful *Alden Besse*, a Maine-built wooden bark that plied the Pacific until she ignominiously ended her days at the port in the late 1920s as a coal barge for the U.S. Navy. (Courtesy of the Allan Knight Collection, Monterey Maritime and History Museum.)

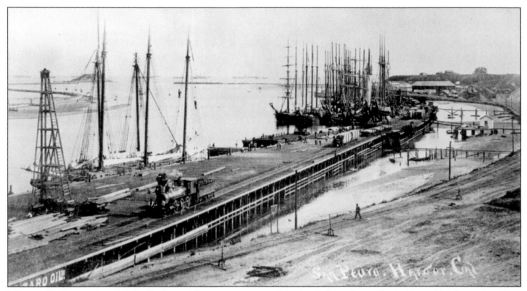

MAIN CHANNEL, 1890. Sailing schooners, some berthed four deep, line the wharf on the San Pedro side of the harbor's Main Channel as Southern Pacific locomotives shuttle lumber-laden flatcars. By this time, lumber from the Pacific Northwest topped the list of commodity cargoes handled at the harbor. (Courtesy of the Port of Los Angeles Archive.)

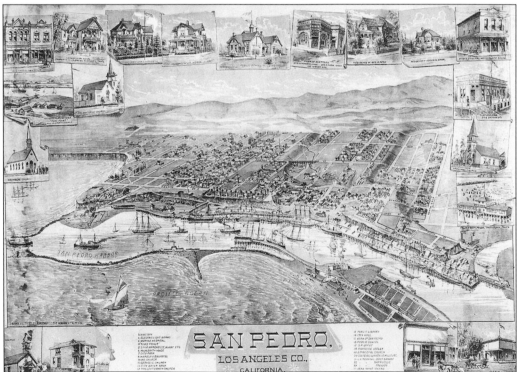

SAN PEDRO, 1892. A view of San Pedro and the harbor in the days before aerial photography shows a general layout with prominent buildings and other points including the Southern Pacific and Los Angeles Terminal Railway depots and wharves, the San Pedro City Hall, the Harbor View Hotel, and the Bank of San Pedro. (Courtesy of the Sherman Library.)

Two

THE GREAT
"FREE HARBOR" FIGHT

In just 45 years, from 1845 to 1890, Los Angeles morphed from a sleepy pueblo of adobe haciendas and meandering dirt streets into a bustling, quasi-respectable city. From a population of 650 in 1846, Los Angeles had grown to more than 50,400 residents in 1890—a figure that would more than double by the end of the decade and triple within another 10 years.

As small communities popped up like weeds across the landscape, the economy, which had largely rested for generations on cattle hides and tallow, surged as well, with sprawling ranchos gradually giving way to citrus orchards, dairy farms, cornfields, small manufacturers, mills, and retail operations.

By the early 1890s, the unprecedented growth made it obvious that there was a critical need for a deepwater harbor to serve the burgeoning Los Angeles region. San Francisco, some 300 miles to the north, and San Diego, 100 miles to the south, could not be relied upon to serve the region's needs.

So the stage was set for the factions arraying themselves to do battle in what later came to be known as the Great Free Harbor Fight.

On one side were a majority of the general population, the recently formed Los Angeles Chamber of Commerce, and the federal government, all of which wanted to see the harbor develop at San Pedro. On the other were the powerful forces of Collis Huntington's Southern Pacific Railroad and the City of Santa Monica, which wanted to see a deepwater harbor called Port Los Angeles developed farther north, around the Palos Verdes Peninsula, up the coast of San Pedro Bay on the northern arc of Santa Monica Bay.

By 1897, the hard-fought, seven-year battle ended when the Los Angeles Chamber of Commerce faction, led by the indomitable Sen. Stephen M. White, won out with a government-appointed commission ruling that Southern California's primary deepwater harbor should be developed in San Pedro.

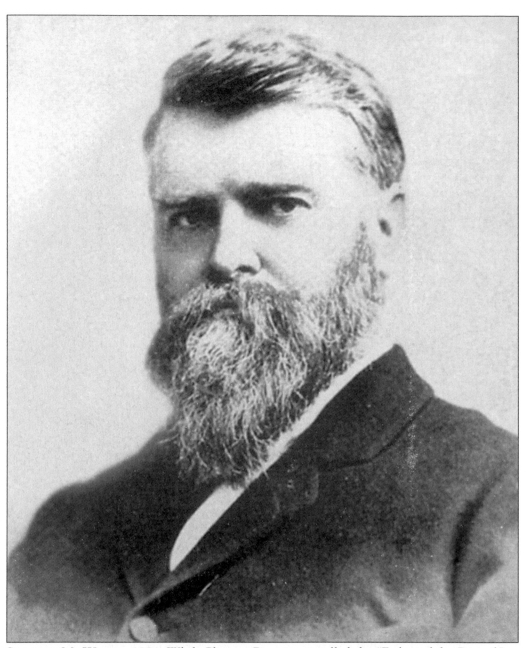

STEPHEN M. WHITE, 1891. While Phineas Banning is called the "Father of the Port of Los Angeles," many consider Sen. Stephen M. White its savior. A California native, White led the pro–San Pedro faction in the Great Free Harbor Fight of the 1890s. Joining him in the political free-for-all were the *Los Angeles Times* and the Los Angeles Chamber of Commerce. He won the hard-fought battle on the floor of the U.S. Senate but didn't live to see the fruits of his success. White died in 1901 at the age of 48, just six years before the Port of Los Angeles was officially created. (Author's collection.)

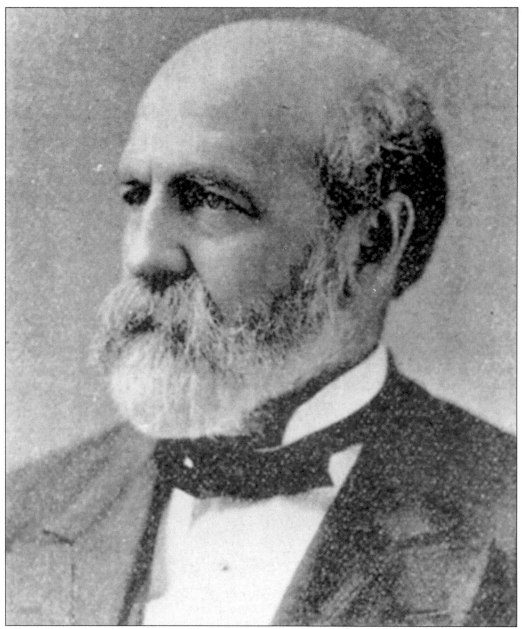

COLLIS HUNTINGTON, 1891. Arrayed against the pro–San Pedro Harbor faction were the considerable forces of railroad mogul Collis Huntington, chairman of the Southern Pacific Railroad and highly influential advocate of a deepwater harbor at nearby Santa Monica. Sen. William Frye of Maine, a vocal supporter of the Santa Monica interests, carried the flag in Washington, where he exerted considerable influence as chairman of the powerful Senate Commerce Committee. (Author's collection.)

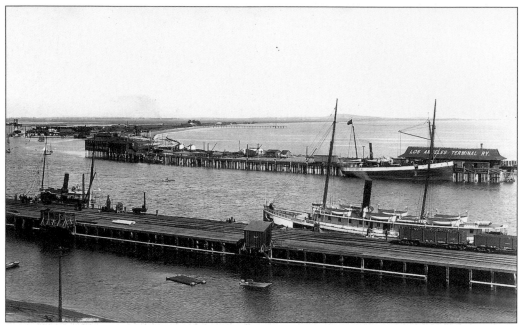

LOS ANGELES TERMINAL RAILWAY, 1892. The upstart Los Angeles Terminal Railway (LATR) was created by a group of St. Louis businessmen to link Los Angeles and the harbor in competition with the Southern Pacific Railroad. The new line linked the mainland with a deepwater terminal on the south end of Rattlesnake Island, later Terminal Island. (Courtesy of the Port of Los Angeles Archive.)

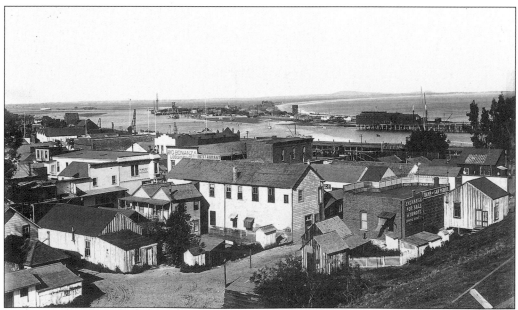

SAN PEDRO, 1893. San Pedro, prior to the growth surge of the late 1890s, resembled nothing more than a sleepy frontier town. The Big Bonanza Hotel (center) provided hospitality for travelers visiting San Pedro, while the Bank of San Pedro (center, right) provided financial security to the town's 2,500 residents. (Courtesy of the Port of Los Angeles Archive.)

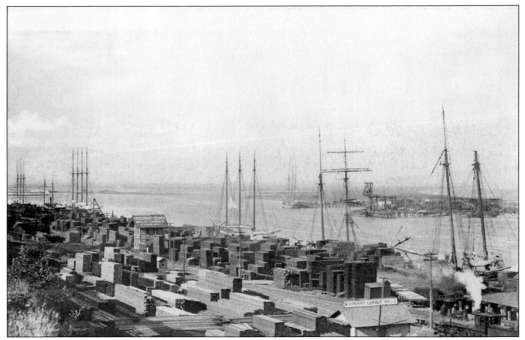

LUMBER WHARF, 1895. The W. H. Perry Lumber Company and the Kerckhoff Mill and Lumber Company yards can be seen in the foreground as several ships unload their cargoes. By this time, lumber from the Pacific Northwest was second only to petroleum as the port's primary trade commodity. (Courtesy of the Title Insurance and Trust Collection, University of Southern California.)

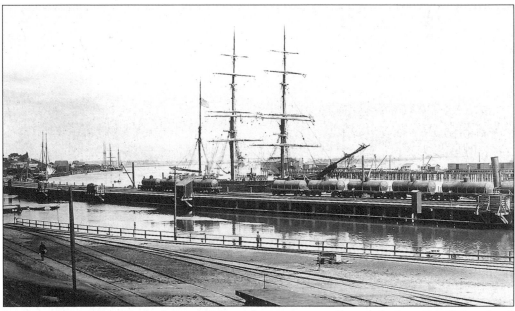

LOADING OIL, 1896. The bark *Enoch Talbot* takes on a cargo of barreled oil at a San Pedro wharf. Ironically the *Enoch Talbot* ended her days as a U.S. Navy coal barge and was abandoned in 1924. By the dawn of the 20th century, the region's burgeoning petroleum industry began accounting for a significant amount of business at the harbor. (Courtesy of the Sherman Library.)

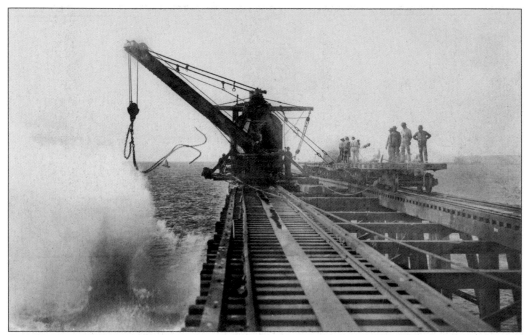

BUILDING THE BREAKWATER, 1899. A rail line was built on trestles parallel to the proposed breakwater, giving rail cars carrying rock and equipment access to the work site. Much of the rock used in the construction was quarried on Santa Catalina Island and carried to San Pedro by barge. The first 8,500-foot section of the breakwater was completed in 1911. (Courtesy of the Title Trust and Insurance Collection, University of Southern California.)

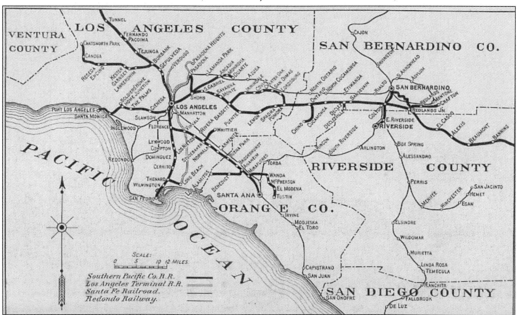

RAIL NETWORK, 1902. At the turn of the 20th century, four railroads—the Southern Pacific, the Pacific Electric, the Los Angeles Terminal Railway, and the Redondo Railway—connected the harbor at San Pedro with points in four Southern California counties. They also offered connecting services with other railroads to major business centers across the country. (Author's collection.)

24

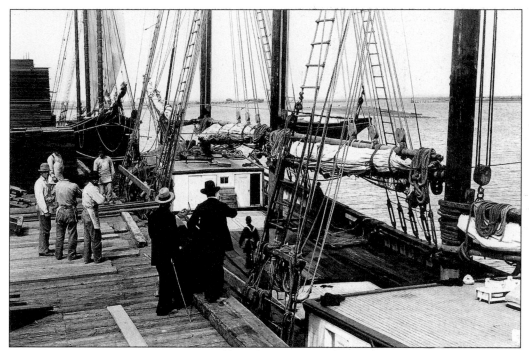

UNLOADING LUMBER, 1902. A gang of longshoremen stands by as two managers supervise the unloading of an unidentified, two-mast coastal schooner at the Hammond Lumber Company wharf. More than a half-dozen lumber companies operated terminals on the busy San Pedro waterfront. (Courtesy of the Port of Los Angeles Archive.)

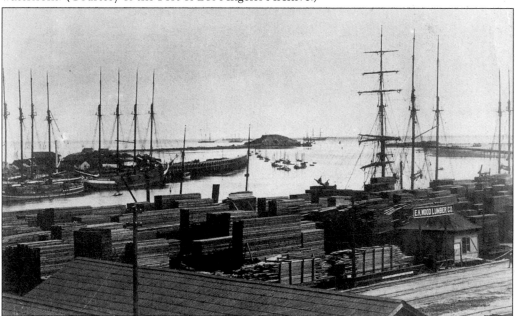

E. K. WOOD LUMBER COMPANY, 1903. A three-mast barentine unloads its cargo of cut lumber at the E. K. Wood Lumber Company wharf on the San Pedro side of the Main Channel, while a pair of four-masted schooners berthed bow to stern across the Main Channel do the same. Within 10 years, the port was the busiest lumber port in the world. (Author's collection.)

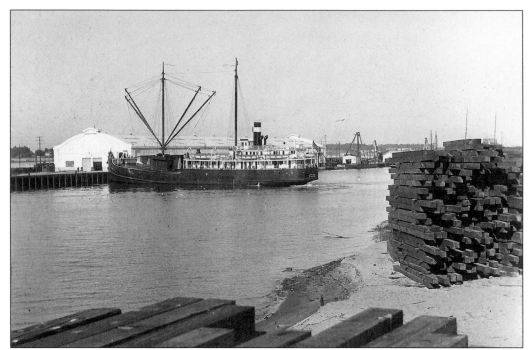

LUMBER SCHOONERS, 1907. Steam-powered schooners, known as "sea-going steam kettles," handled much of the lumber moving from the Puget Sound and the Columbia River to Southern California in the early years of the 20th century (above). The *Alice Blanchard* (below) was a typical example of the ships that made up what was called the "Scandinavian Navy" because of the preponderance of Swedes, Danes, and Norwegians that comprised their crews. Only one example of the once-ubiquitous lumber schooners exists today—the *Wapama*, which is preserved at the National Maritime Museum Park in San Francisco. (Both courtesy of the Sherman Library.)

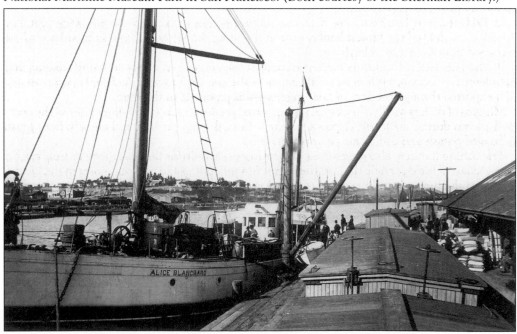

Three

LUMBER, ORANGES, AND STEEL SHIPS

Developments at the Port of Los Angeles in the years following its official creation in 1907, up to the start of World War II, were far-reaching in their sweep and foundational in their impact on the port's future.

Improvements to the port's infrastructure—the creation of the breakwater and several major dredging projects—advanced at a breathless pace, while new wharves and terminals were built to serve the increasing number of shipping lines that connected Southern California with import-export markets around the world.

In 1911, the port handled more than one million barrels of oil, and the following year, Los Angeles was dubbed the busiest lumber port in the world, handling millions of board feet of cut softwood from the Pacific Northwest.

By the late 1920s, California ranked second in the country in terms of manufacturing and petroleum production, while close to 30 percent of the country's total agricultural output—much of it exported through the Port of Los Angeles—was produced in the state.

Millions of dollars worth of imported and exported products and commodities crossed the port's docks, even during the tough Depression years—from Belgian pig iron and raw silk from Japan to bagged potash and California-grown citrus fruit.

The fishing industry also played a major part in port activity as the processing of tuna caught off the coast of Mexico made the port the largest fish processing and packing center in the United States, while shipyards at the port turned out dozens of freighters, tankers, and auxiliary craft for private shipping lines and the military both before and during World War II.

But perhaps the most significant development wasn't at the port itself but 2,951 miles to the south in Central America, where the opening of the Panama Canal in 1914 made the port a global competitor by virtually guaranteeing increased cargo volumes generated not only by the United States' intercoastal trades, but to import-export markets in the Caribbean, the Mediterranean, and Northern Europe that had historically been dominated by U.S. East Coast and Gulf of Mexico ports.

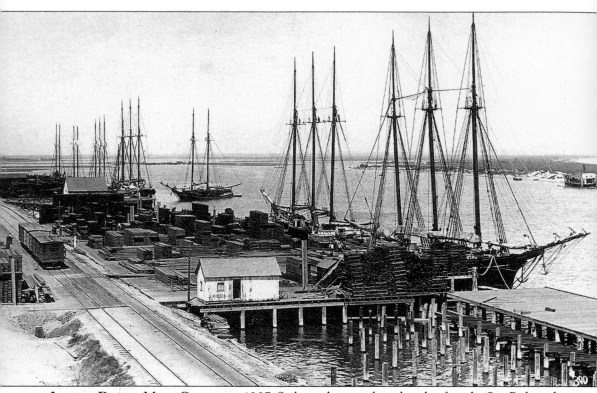

LUMBER DOCK—MAIN CHANNEL, 1907. Sailing schooners line the wharf on the San Pedro side of the harbor's Main Channel. Just a few months after this photograph was taken, the harbor, known for decades simply as San Pedro, officially became the Port of Los Angeles. (Courtesy of the Sherman Library.)

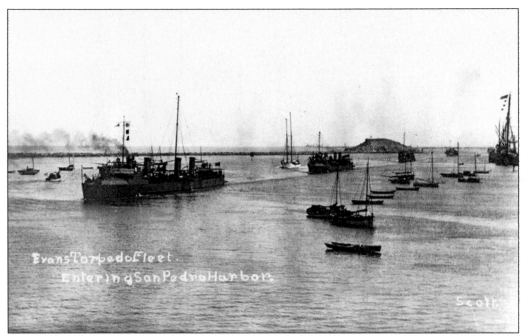

GREAT WHITE FLEET, 1908. Four large torpedo boat destroyers of Adm. Robley Evans's torpedo boat flotilla can be seen entering the port's Main Channel with Deadman's Island and the partially completed breakwater in the background. The fleet called at the port on April 18 and departed a few days later for San Francisco and the Orient. (Courtesy of the Title Insurance and Trust Collection, University of Southern California.)

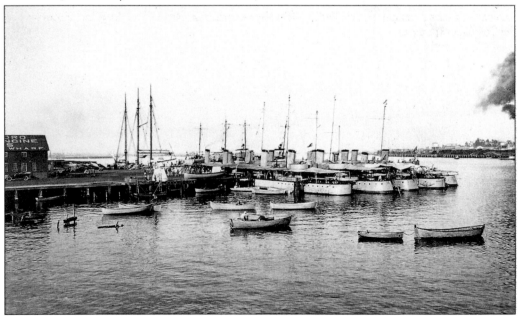

ENGINE WORKSHOP, 1910. The San Pedro Engine Works was one of scores of companies at the port providing specialized equipment, supplies, fuel, and repairs to vessels of all sizes from rowboats to battleships. A three-masted schooner and several unidentified U.S. Navy craft can be seen here nested at the company's facility. (Courtesy of the Port of Los Angeles Archive.)

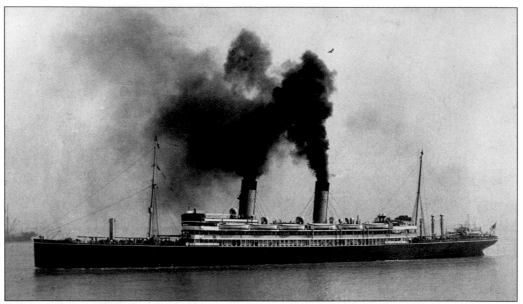

SHINYO MARU, 1911. The *Shinyo Maru* was one of three sister ships operated by Japan's Toyo Kisen Kaisha (TKK) on the company's route linking Los Angeles and San Francisco with Japan and the Far East. Unable to compete with larger steamship companies from both Japan and the United States, TKK was absorbed by Tokyo-based Nippon Yusen Kaisha (NYK) in 1926. (Courtesy of the Allan Knight Collection, Monterey Maritime and History Museum.)

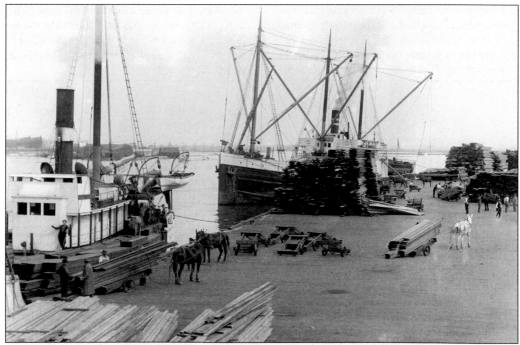

LUMBER MULES, 1912. For many years, hardworking mules were used to haul cargo at several of the port's busiest lumber terminals. Teams are busy moving cut wood from pier side to storage at the Southern California Lumber Company's yard at Berth 229. (Courtesy of the Port of Los Angeles Archive.)

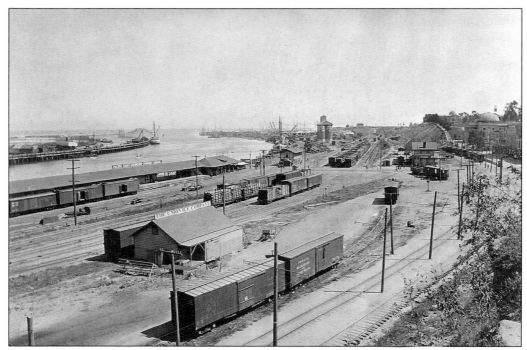

SOUTHERN PACIFIC RAILYARD, 1912. The Southern Pacific Railroad provided a key service connecting the growing port and points across the country. The company's yard covered all of the flat ground below the bluff south of Seventh Street in San Pedro (above). The Union Ice House, which supplied the ice for refrigerated railcars, is at the center. Another view a few years later (below) shows the yard turntable, a pair of locomotives, and boxcars from an assortment of railroads including the Rock Island, Illinois Central, St. Paul & Des Moines, and Chicago & Northwestern. (Both courtesy of the Port of Los Angeles Archive.)

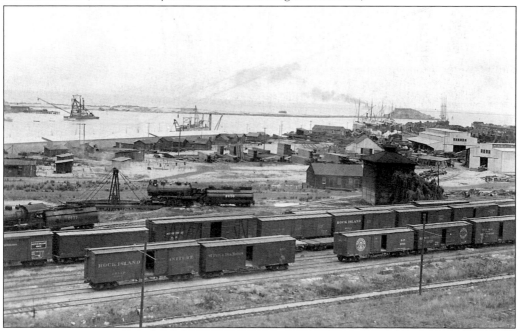

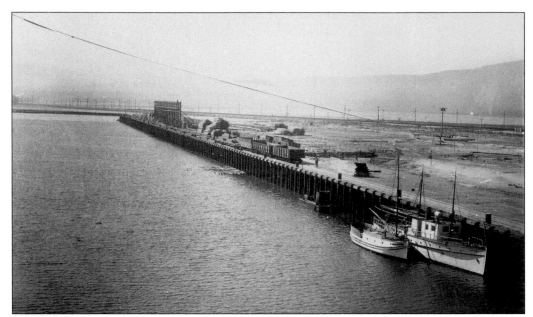

TRANSIT SHED CONSTRUCTION, 1913. The surge in growth at the port necessitated the development of new facilities and infrastructure, including piers, wharves, warehouses, and rail lines. Here workmen have just started the framing of the new transit shed at Berths 156–158 on Pier A. Rail cars are positioned on dockside rails, while lumber is stacked nearby. (Author's collection.)

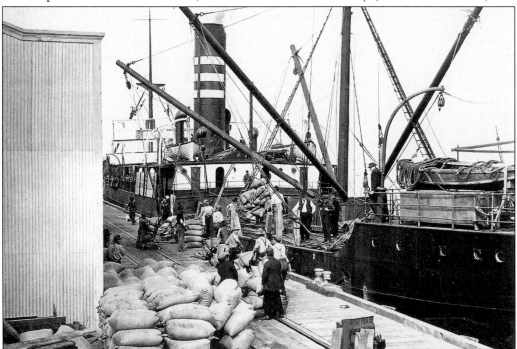

CARGO FOR EXPORT, 1913. A variety of cargo is seen being loaded aboard an unidentified Mitsui Line freighter for shipment to Japan and the Orient. Mitsui Line and its many counterparts helped greatly in developing the new Port of Los Angeles into a truly international transportation hub. (Courtesy of the Sherman Library.)

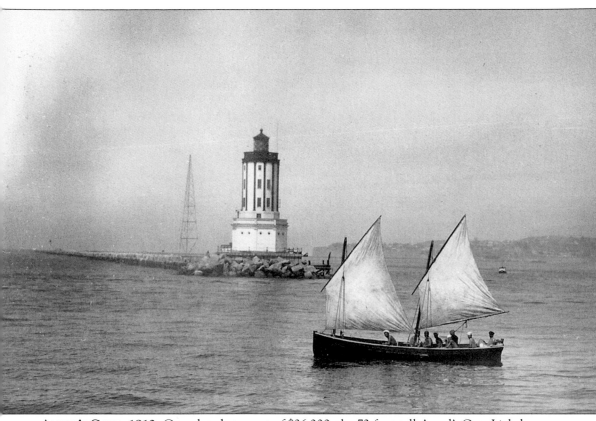

ANGEL'S GATE, 1913. Completed at a cost of $36,000, the 73-foot-tall Angel's Gate Lighthouse was built at the end of the 9,250-foot breakwater to mark the entrance to the port. The steel and concrete lighthouse is still operational and has survived innumerable hazards, including a five-day storm in 1939 that sent massive waves smashing into the structure. (Courtesy of the Title Insurance and Trust Collection, University of Southern California.)

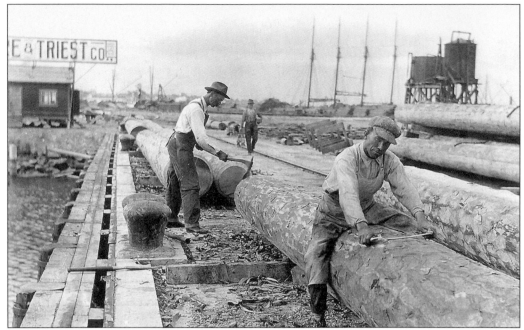

PIER CONSTRUCTION, 1914. Work on the port's first municipal pier was completed by hundreds of workmen, two of whom can be seen preparing one of the scores of wharf piles used in the project. After finishing, the piles were pounded into the muddy floor of the Main Channel by giant steam-powered, barge-mounted drivers. The wharf was initially used by the American-Hawaiian Steamship Company. (Courtesy of the Sherman Library.)

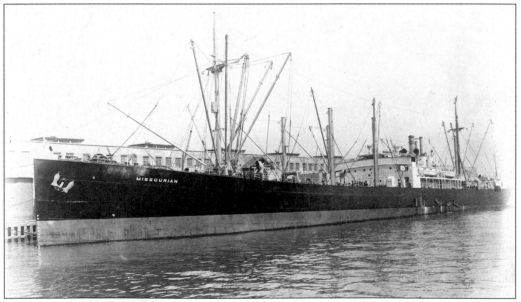

SS MISSOURIAN, 1914. The U.S.-flag *Missourian* was the first cargo ship to visit the Port of Los Angeles after the opening of the Panama Canal. The full impact of the opening of the canal on the port wasn't realized until seven years later when the canal was reopened to commercial service following the end of World War I. (Courtesy of the Allan Knight Collection, Monterey Maritime and History Museum.)

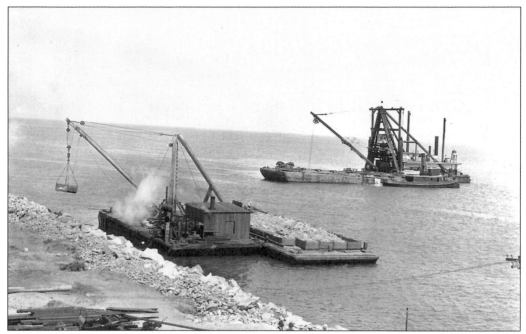

HARBOR IMPROVEMENTS, 1915. Work on dredging the Main Channel included removing silt buildup and dumping more rock to widen the jetty linking Rattlesnake Island and Deadman's Island. These activities continued simultaneously through the year. The jetty was eventually expanded to form a major extension of Terminal Island. (Courtesy of the Sherman Library.)

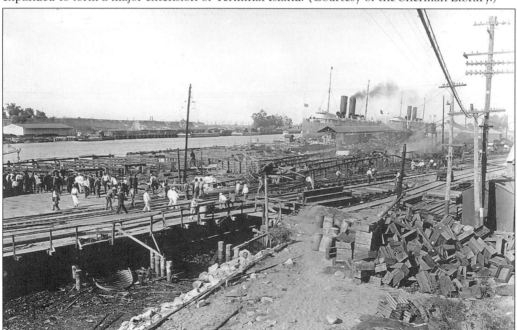

YALE-HARVARD FIRE, 1915. A fire completely destroyed the Los Angeles Steamship Company wharf used by the coastal liners *Harvard* and *Yale* and burned for the better part of a day before it was extinguished. The two ships can be seen in the background as interested San Pedro residents gather to watch the wharf smolder. (Courtesy of the Sherman Library.)

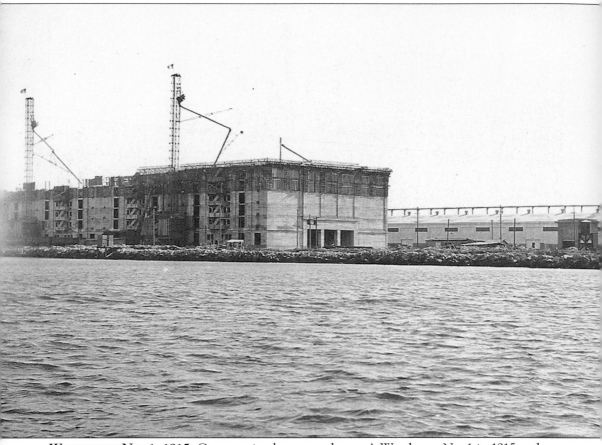

WAREHOUSE NO. 1, 1915. Construction began on the port's Warehouse No. 1 in 1915 and was completed two years later. The building was the largest structure of its kind at the port when it was erected and is still in use 90 years later. For a time, it was the only customs-bonded warehouse at the Port of Los Angeles. (Courtesy of the Sherman Library.)

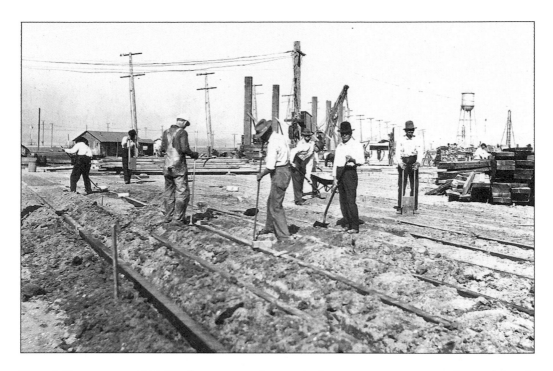

PIER A EXTENSION, 1916. Workers prepare the site for the concrete extension to Pier A (above), while a crane dumps a load of rock for the project (below). The work was financed by the city's first $3-million harbor improvement bond and included a new reinforced wharf at Berths 57–60 in the East Basin as well as the paving of a street leading to Warehouse No. 1. The construction of new wharves and improvements to existing berths dominated activity at the port for several years in anticipation of surges in cargo volumes. (Both courtesy of the Sherman Library.)

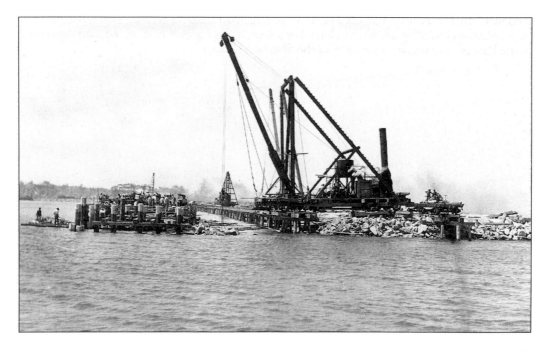

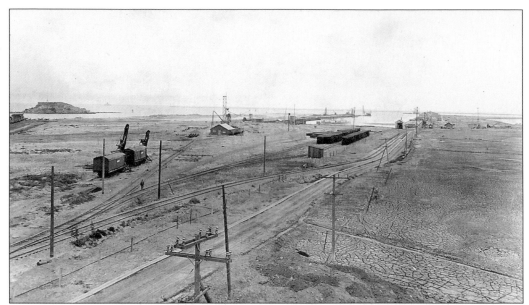

MUDFLATS, 1916. Deadman's Island looms to the left across the Main Channel as dredging and wharf construction proceeds in the far distance. Building materials, including stacks of railroad ties, sit ready as an expanse of empty mudflats awaits the continued development of the sprawling port. (Courtesy of the Sherman Library.)

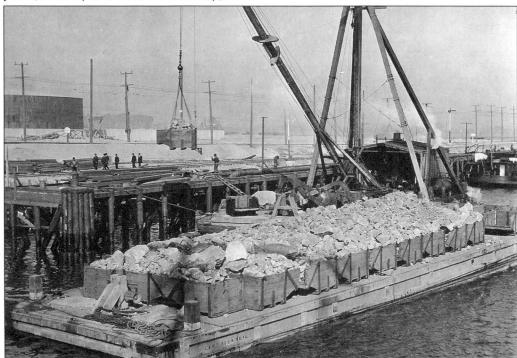

OIL DOCK CONSTRUCTION, 1916. The petroleum business had gained a major foothold in the port in the days prior to World War I. The Standard Oil Company dock was built near the Main Channel Turning Basin and could handle two tankers at the same time. The facility also had storage space for 460,000 barrels of oil on-site. (Courtesy of the Sherman Library.)

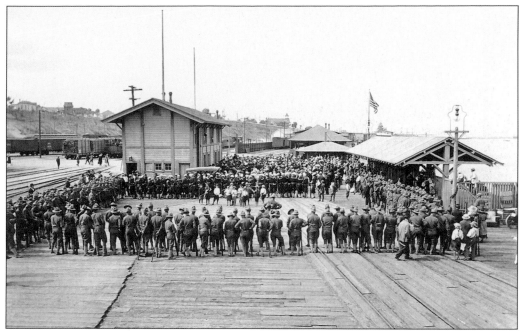

JOINT OPERATIONS, 1917. Though the Great War was being fought thousands of miles away in Europe, the military took advantage of the port's facilities by conducting early-era, joint-service exercises. A formation of fully equipped U.S. Marines and sailors stand at ease as an audience of young San Pedro residents gathers to watch. (Courtesy of the Port of Los Angeles Archive.)

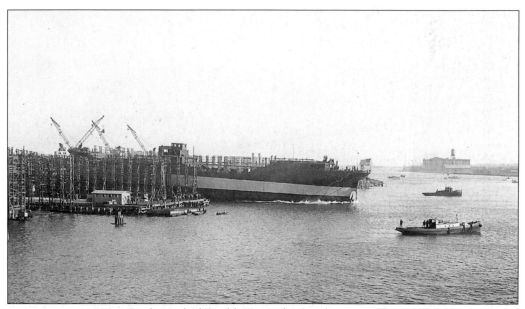

SHIP LAUNCH, 1918. By the end of World War I, the Southwestern Shipbuilding Company on Terminal Island had built 19 cargo ships and six tankers for the U.S. Shipping Board at its yard at Berth 240. A freighter can be seen sliding down the yard's ways into the port's Main Channel. The Southwestern facility was acquired by the Bethlehem Shipbuilding Corporation in 1922. (Courtesy of the Sherman Library.)

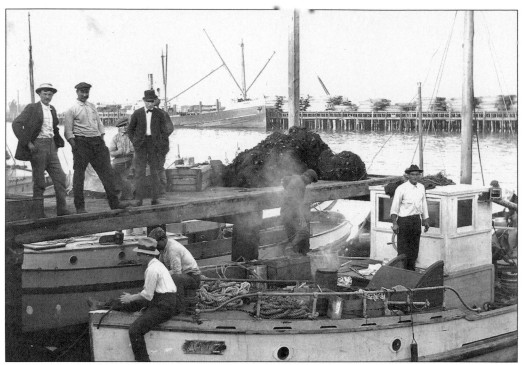

FISHING BOATS, 1919. The destruction of the California Fish Company processing plant by fire in 1914 spurred the development of Fish Harbor, which became the center of the port's vibrant deep-sea fishing and canning industry. Some of the 400 fishing boats working out of the port anchor side by side (below). Fishermen clean their boat after unloading their sardine catch (above). One of the largest operations at the port was the French Sardine Company, which later became Star-Kist Foods and pioneered the use of crushed ice to keep fish fresh. (Both courtesy of the Sherman Library.)

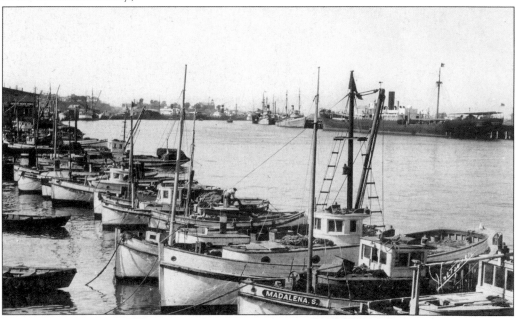

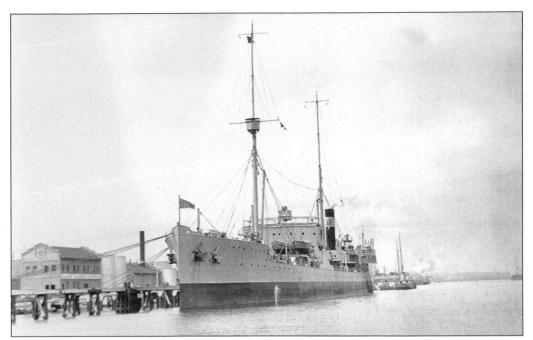

LOADING FUEL OIL, 1919. An unidentified U.S. Navy tanker takes on a load of fuel oil for the fleet. The low cost of fuel, thanks to the port's proximity to several major Southern California oil refineries and its easily accessible terminals, made it a major port-of-call for ships needing to inexpensively refill their bunkers. (Courtesy of the Sherman Library.)

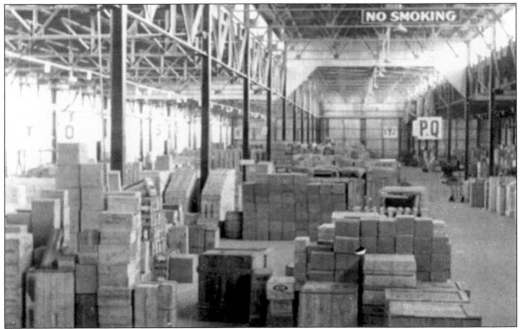

WAREHOUSE NO. 1, INTERIOR, 1920. The six-story, concrete warehouse covers almost 478,000 square feet of storage space, as well as access for both railcars and trucks. The building served for years as the original home of the port's Marine Exchange, which operated an observation and signaling station on the roof. (Courtesy of the Sherman Library.)

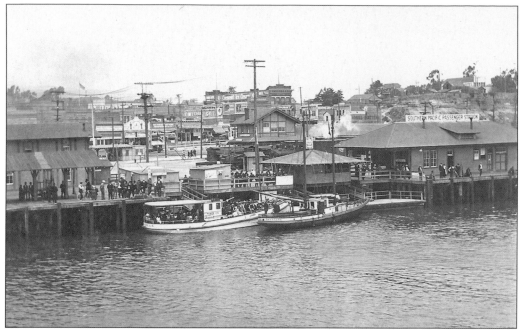

FOOT OF SIXTH STREET, 1920. A group of small boats congregates to ferry passengers across the Main Channel from San Pedro to Terminal Island. The location was later the site of the Municipal Ferry Building, which offered service for cars and passengers on the 10-minute trip across the Main Channel between San Pedro and Terminal Island. (Courtesy of the Sherman Library.)

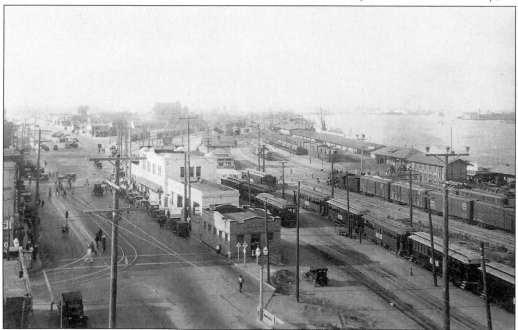

FRONT STREET, SAN PEDRO, 1921. San Pedro sprawls into the distant early-morning haze as pedestrians cross the Pacific Electric tracks on Front Street to the interurban Red Cars lining up at the station. A freight train slowly steams through the yard, past the transit sheds and wharves lining the Main Channel to the right. (Courtesy of the Sherman Library.)

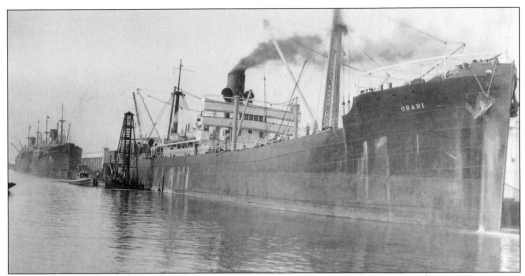

WEST COAST'S BUSIEST PORT, 1920. The Port of Los Angeles defied its detractors when it surpassed San Francisco as the busiest port on the U.S. West Coast and ranked second to New York in terms of export tonnage. The rust-streaked freighter *Orani* can be seen building up a head of steam before casting off from her berth. (Author's collection.)

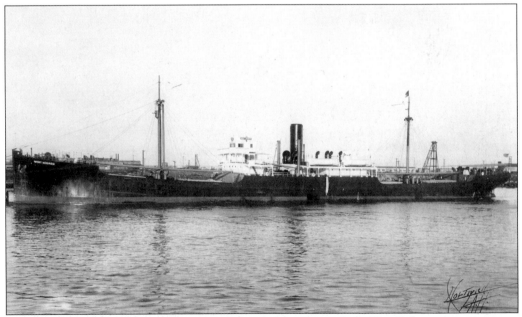

ECONOMIC IMPACT, 1921. The States Steamship Company cargo liner *West Kedron* is seen underway in the Main Channel with an export cargo for China and the Far East. A contemporary report by the University of Southern California and three Los Angeles–area banks stated that the port contributed more than $100 million to the local economy, based on activities either directly or indirectly related to operations at the harbor. (Author's collection.)

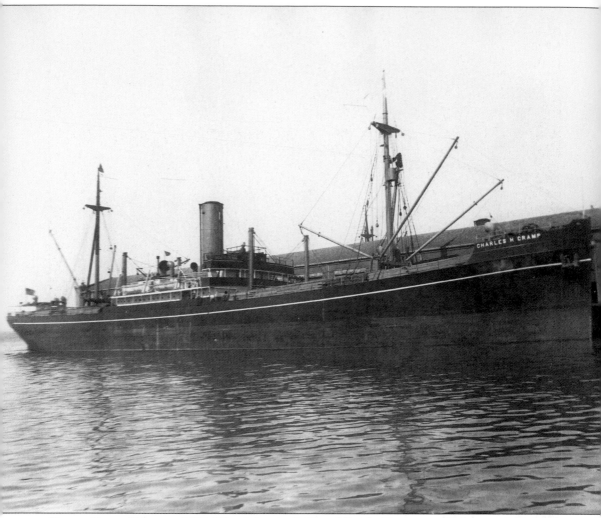

CITRUS FRUIT EXPRESS, 1921. The Atlantic, Gulf, and Pacific Company of Baltimore, Maryland, invested $2 million in a venture to transport California-grown citrus fruit and cotton to ports along the U.S. Gulf and East Coasts. The company acquired six ships totaling 55,000 deadweight tons for the operation from the U.S. Shipping Board. The service was the first of its kind between coasts via ship through the Panama Canal. One of the six ships employed in the trade was the 9,400-ton *Charles H. Cramp.* The vessel, affectionately known as "The Sunkist Queen," was the first ship to sail on the new service. (Courtesy of the Allan Knight Collection, Monterey Maritime and History Museum.)

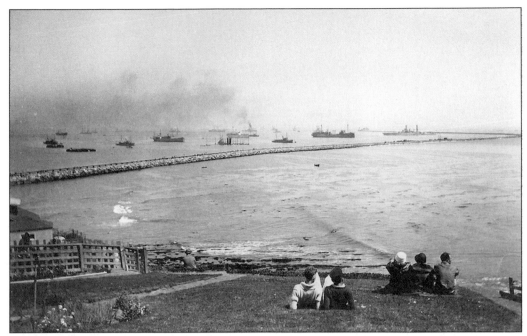

SHIP WATCHING, 1921. Picnickers on the bluff near Point Fermin enjoy a panoramic view of ships anchored inside the breakwater on a lazy Sunday afternoon. In the years when the number of ships calling at Los Angeles exceeded the port's capacity to handle them, many ships had to anchor inside the breakwater, waiting for a berth to load or unload their cargoes. (Courtesy of the Sherman Library.)

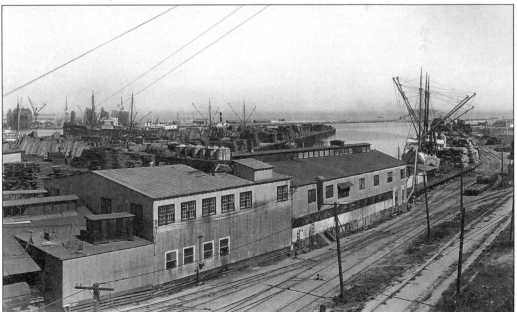

S. P. SLIP, 1922. The slip, located near what is now Berths 91–93 on the Main Channel at the far south end of Ports O' Call Village, was the former site of Timms Landing. In the years before a regular schoolhouse was built in San Pedro, the original warehouse at the landing served that purpose with classes for 15 pupils. (Courtesy of the Sherman Library.)

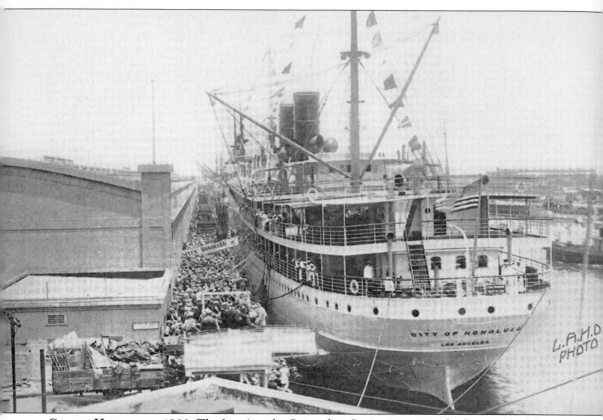

CITY OF HONOLULU, 1922. The Los Angeles Steamship Company acquired a German-built liner for use on its route linking the Port of Los Angeles and Honolulu. The ship was to operate on a joint service with the liner *City of Los Angeles*. Sadly the *City of Honolulu* was lost in September 1922 on the return leg of her first voyage to her namesake when a fire broke out in the ship's second-class dining saloon and spread throughout the ship. All 74 passengers and 187 crew members aboard were saved through the efforts of several merchant and U.S. Navy ships that answered the distress call. The incident was later dubbed the "Shipwreck Deluxe" as the chief steward had provisioned the ship's lifeboats with roast chicken and other delicacies, as well as cigarettes and plenty to drink . . . besides water. (Courtesy of the Port of Los Angeles Archive.)

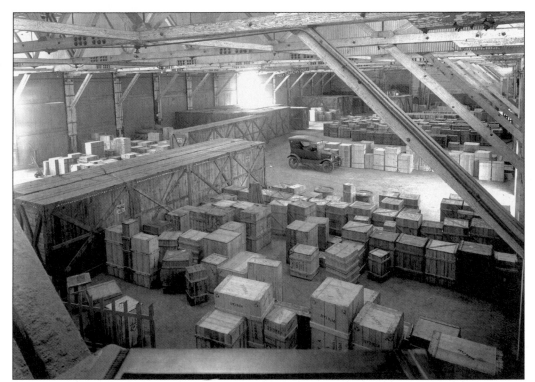

TRANSIT SHED INTERIOR, 1923. The interior of a high-beamed transit shed at the port is seen here with a wide variety of crated cargo laid out and sorted for transshipment. Dominating the scene are several disassembled airplanes that have been boxed for shipment overseas and dwarf the photographer's Model A Ford. (Courtesy of the Port of Los Angeles Archive.)

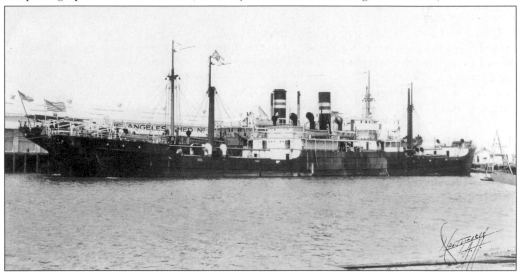

U.S. SHIPPING BOARD, 1923. The federal government agency was created in 1917 to help put the nation's merchant marine on an equal footing with the globe-traversing merchant fleets of Great Britain, Japan, Germany, and the Netherlands. The agency oversaw the building of scores of freighters including the freighter *West Notus*, which sailed from the port on the McCormick Steamship's Pacific-Argentine-Brazil Line service. (Author's collection.)

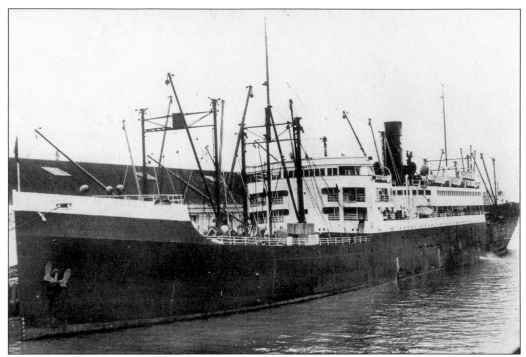

PRESIDENT MONROE, 1924. The *President Monroe* was one of seven ships that the Dollar Steamship Company operated on a twice-monthly, round-the-world service under the terms of a mail contract with the U.S. Shipping Board. The ship, a "502"-type passenger-cargo liner, called at Los Angeles before sailing on to 22 ports via San Francisco. (Author's collection.)

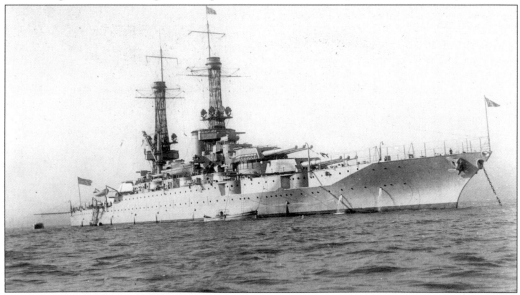

BATTLESHIP EXPLOSION, 1924. The port became the headquarters for the U.S. Pacific Fleet in 1922. Two years later, the battleship USS *Mississippi* suffered an explosion in one of her 14-inch gun turrets that killed 56 sailors during gunnery practice off Santa Catalina Island. More than 10,000 people turned out for the service held at nearby Fort MacArthur for the men lost. (Courtesy of the Allan Knight Collection, Monterey Maritime and History Museum.)

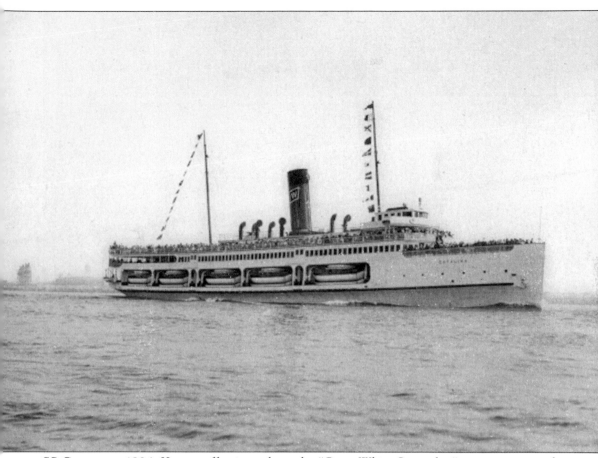

SS CATALINA, 1924. Known affectionately as the "Great White Steamship" to generations of Southern Californians, the steamship *Catalina* plied the 26-mile stretch of water between the Port of Los Angeles and Avalon on Santa Catalina Island, daily for 51 years, except for her time as a U.S. Army transport during World War II. The mayor of Los Angeles, George Cryer, and 3,000 visitors were on hand for her launching at the Los Angeles Shipbuilding and Drydock Company yard in San Pedro. The ship carried more than 25 million passengers in her career, more than have been carried by any other ship of any type or size in history. In the 1950s, the round-trip fare was $3.26 each way, tax included. The SS *Catalina* was withdrawn from service in 1975, and as of this writing her hulk lies rusting at the port of Ensenada, Mexico. (Author's collection.)

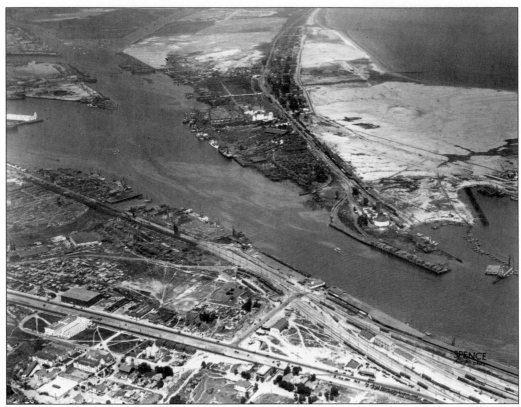

MAIN CHANNEL, 1925. Looking northeast, this aerial shot of the Port of Los Angeles shows the port's Turning Basin and West Basin with the Los Angeles Shipbuilding and Drydock Company in the right center foreground. Several ships are tied up along the Main Channel, and to the right Terminal Island awaits further development. (Author's collection.)

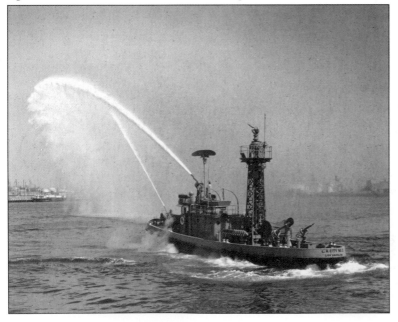

L.A. CITY FIREBOAT NO. 2, 1925. The fireboat *L.A. City No. 2*, also known as the *Ralph J. Scott*, was built in 1925 at the Los Angeles Shipbuilding and Drydock Company yard in San Pedro at a cost of $214,000. The boat fought several of the port's largest ship fires and remained in service until her retirement in the early 1980s. (Author's collection.)

BERTH 159, 1925. On a typically busy day at one of the port's busiest wharves, a Williams Line steamer is dockside while stacks of bagged cargo, barrels, and an export shipment of farm tractors and other equipment wait to be loaded for shipment to unknown foreign fields. More than 140 ships flying the flags of 13 countries called at the port during the year. (Courtesy of the Sherman Library.)

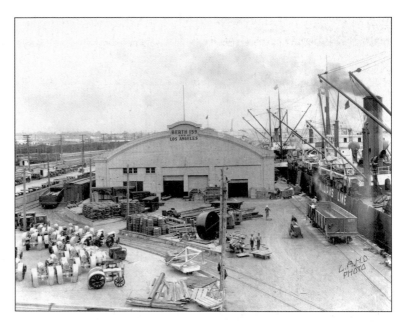

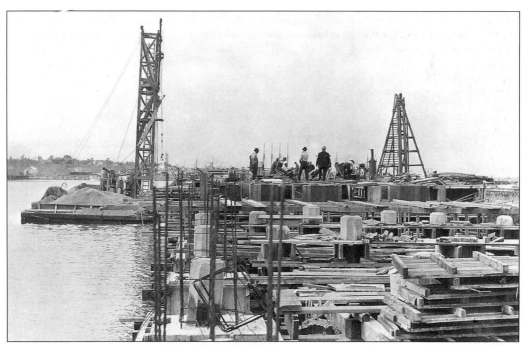

ONGOING CONSTRUCTION, 1925. Building new piers and wharves and the long-needed widening of the Main Channel to 1,000 feet were the dominant infrastructure activities at the port in the 1920s. By 1925, an extension of the breakwater was added that extended it to 4.5 miles. (Courtesy of the Sherman Library.)

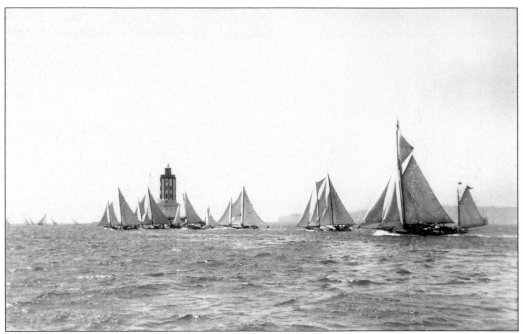

YACHT RACES, 1925. The Los Angeles Yacht Club was founded in 1901 as the South Coast Yacht Club and every year held its San Pedro–Santa Barbara yacht race. The race, which drew competitors from up and down the West Coast, began with a run past the Angel's Gate Lighthouse. (Courtesy of the Newport Harbor Nautical Museum.)

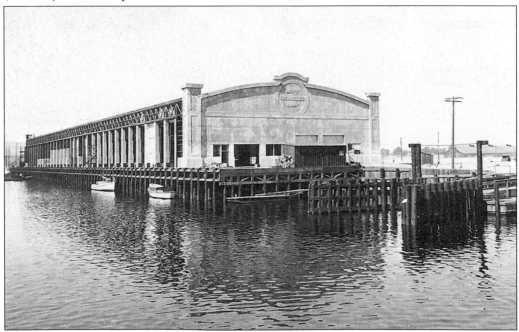

WATER STREET WHARF, 1926. Located at the foot of Water Street in Wilmington, the concrete warehouse was built on the site of Phineas Banning's original wooden wharf, not far from the current site of the Trans Pacific Container Service Corporation's container terminal. (Courtesy of the Port of Los Angeles Archive.)

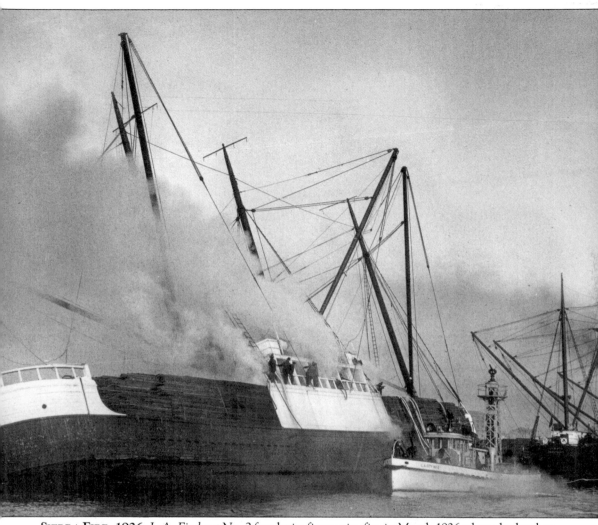

SIERRA FIRE, 1926. *L.A. Fireboat No. 2* fought its first major fire in March 1926 when the lumber schooner *Sierra* caught on fire and burned at the E. K. Wood Lumber Company wharf. Quick action by firemen and dockworkers to move stacks of lumber piled on the dock away from the burning ship was credited with helping to control the spread of the blaze. (Courtesy of the Los Angeles Fire Department Museum.)

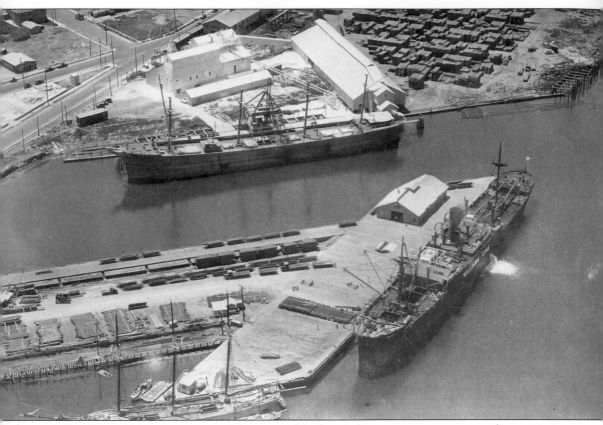

A Sad End, 1928. A once-proud four-masted bark, cut down to serve as a storage barge, sits at her last berth as a Williams Line steamer unloads its cargo. In the foreground is a three-masted schooner, a veteran of better days hauling lumber from the Pacific Northwest to feed Southern California's insatiable construction industry. (Author's collection.)

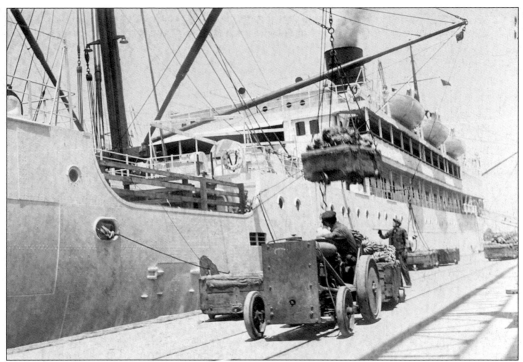

UNLOADING BANANAS, 1928. The port served as the West Coast's primary unloading port for bananas shipped from Central America and the Caribbean. In 1937, off-loading at the port using slings and pallets was replaced by specially-designed conveyor equipment at Berth 147, which permitted rail access for refrigerated rail cars. (Courtesy of the Title Insurance and Trust Collection, University of Southern California.)

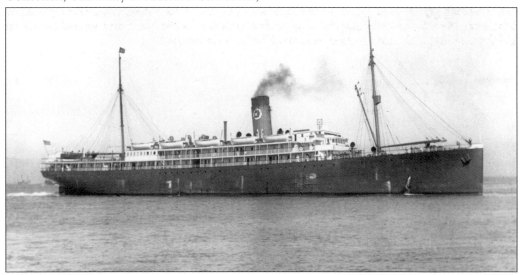

LOS ANGELES-ALASKA LINK, 1929. The stately Pacific Steamship Company liner *Dorothy Alexander* became the first ship to sail on a new service linking the Port of Los Angeles with ports in the Pacific Northwest and Alaska. The Pacific Steamship Company also owned the Admiral Oriental Line, which operated a transpacific service out of Seattle. (Courtesy of the Allan Knight Collection, Monterey Maritime and History Museum.)

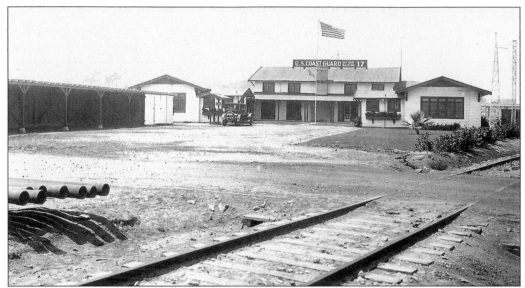

GUARDIANS OF THE PORT, 1929. The U.S. Coast Guard has maintained a presence at the Port of Los Angeles since the port's official inception, performing countless port security and search-and-rescue missions, as well as firefighting, maintaining aids to navigation, performing vessel inspections, and overseeing the cleanup of hazardous material spills. (Courtesy of the Sherman Library.)

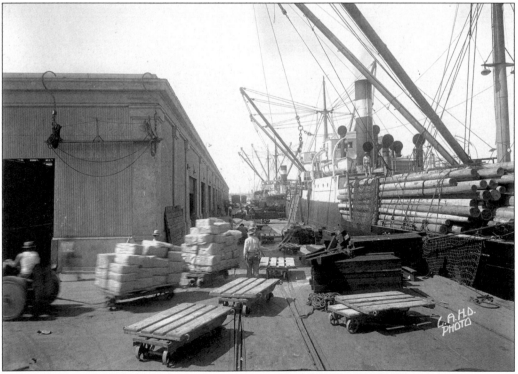

DOCK ACTIVITY, 1929. A tractor pulling wagons of baled freight speeds by in the foreground as the McCormick Steamship Company freighter *Munleon* waits with safety nets rigged for a crew of longshoremen to start unloading the ship's deck cargo of telephone poles. (Courtesy of the Port of Los Angeles Archive.)

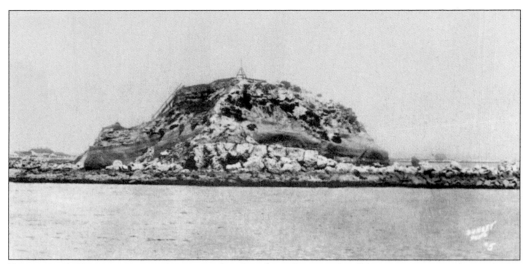

DEADMAN'S ISLAND, 1929. An iconic landmark at the mouth of the port's Main Channel, the towering rock pile marked the entrance to the mouth of the harbor until it was deemed a hazard to navigation and blasted into rubble. Two years of dynamite work finished the job, with the debris used to add 62 acres of landfill to Reservation Point on the southernmost tip of Terminal Island. (Courtesy of the Sherman Library.)

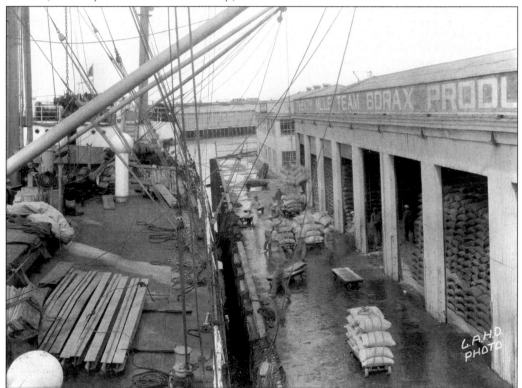

BORAX FOR EXPORT, 1929. More than 55,000 tons of bagged borax valued at $3 million was exported through the Port of Los Angeles during the year. The borax was mined in the Mojave Desert by the U.S. Borax Company and processed at the company's plant in Wilmington. (Courtesy of the Port of Los Angeles Archive.)

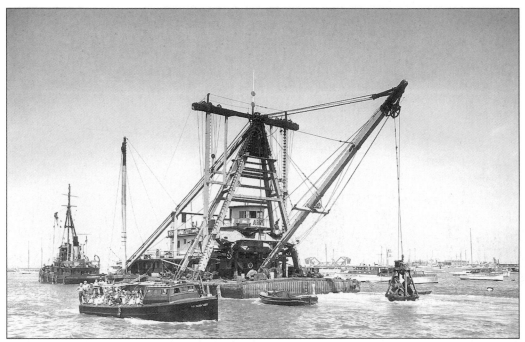

DREDGING, 1930. With the Henry Ford Bridge in the background, work continues on deepening the Cerritos Channel as a water taxi loaded with laborers cruises by. The work was part of a years-long project to dredge the entire harbor to a depth of 35 feet. (Courtesy of the Port of Los Angeles Archive.)

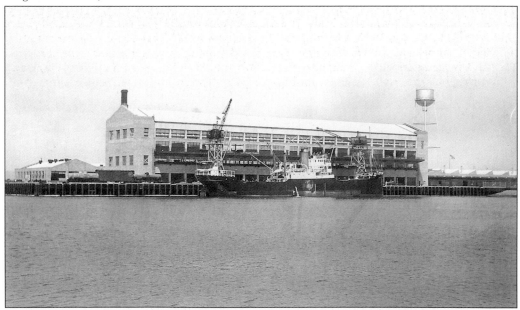

FORD PLANT, 1930. Seeing the developing relationship between Southern Californians and the automobile, Henry Ford opened the doors at a new plant in Wilmington that put 2,000 people to work on its assembly lines. The facility was in a curious position in the port's Cerritos Channel: two-thirds were sited within the Port of Los Angeles with the remaining third in the neighboring Port of Long Beach. (Courtesy of the Sherman Library.)

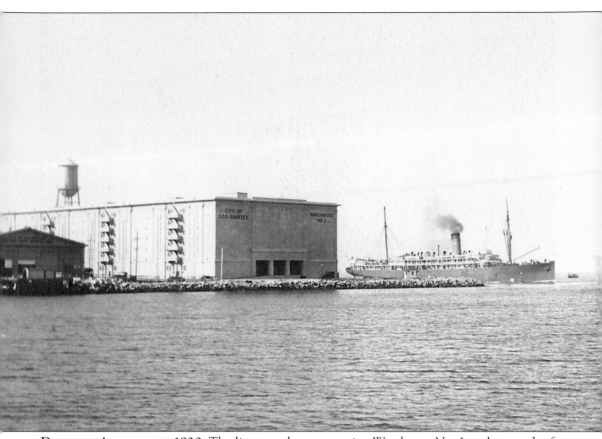

DOROTHY ALEXANDER, 1930. The liner can be seen passing Warehouse No. 1 at the mouth of the Main Channel outbound for San Francisco, Seattle, and Vancouver before calling at Alaska. The *Dorothy Alexander* had accommodations for 294 first-class and 144 second-class passengers and was eventually sold to the Alaska Steamship Company. (Courtesy of the Sherman Library.)

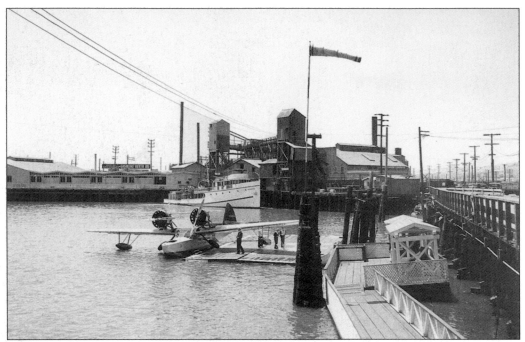

SEAPLANES, 1930. A twin-engine seaplane waits to load passengers at the Catalina Seaplane Terminal in Fish Harbor (above), while several years earlier an open-cockpit seaplane (below) taxis in the Main Channel. In 1928, Allen Field—later taken over by the U.S. Navy and renamed Reeves Field—was built with a seaplane ramp on 410 acres on Terminal Island. Over the years, the port served as a terminus for seaplane operations for several air carriers. In the 1930s, Juan Trippe's Pan American Airways operated a six-plane squadron of giant transpacific clippers from a facility at Reeves Field. (Both courtesy of the Sherman Library.)

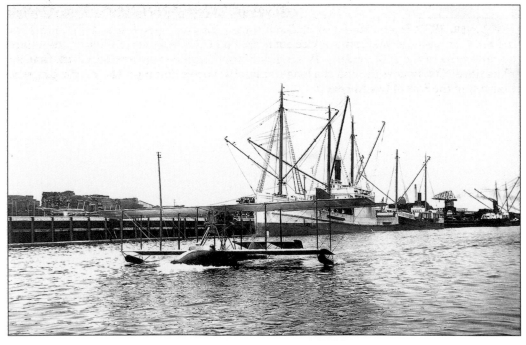

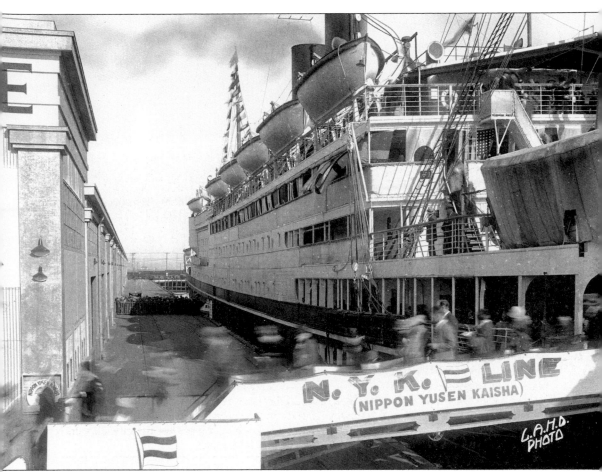

NYK Liner, 1930. Japan's largest steamship company, Nippon Yusen Kaisha (NYK Line) has operated both passenger and cargo service out of the Port of Los Angeles at different times since the early years of the 20th century. Passengers in the foreground swiftly disembark from an unidentified NYK liner at the end of a long transpacific voyage, leaving a blur on the gangway. (Courtesy of the Port of Los Angeles.)

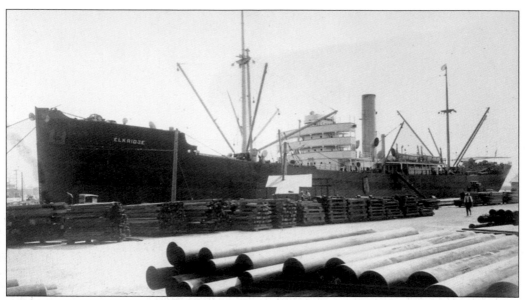

STEEL PIPE IMPORTS, 1930. By the late 1920s, petroleum extraction was one of Southern California's primary industries. The freighter *Elkridge* has just unloaded her cargo of steel pipe for use at one of the refineries located near the port. In 1929 alone, more than 537,000 tons of steel pipe valued at more than $69 million was imported from eight countries through the Port of Los Angeles. (Author's collection.)

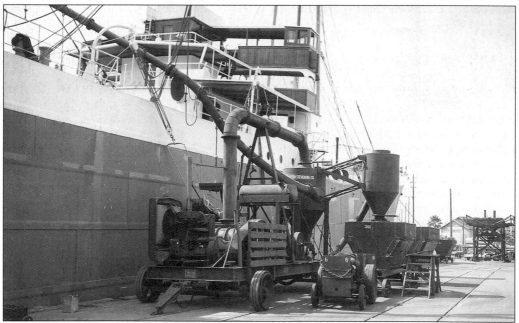

UNLOADING COPRA, 1931. Some cargoes moving through the port weren't shipped in crates, barrels, bags, or bales. Copra imports from Indonesia, India, the Philippines, and elsewhere, for example, required handling with specialized equipment. Shipments of the sun-dried coconut meat—which was used in making margarine and vegetable oil—were unloaded using giant suction vacuums, which deposited the product into waiting bins or railcars. (Courtesy of the Sherman Library.)

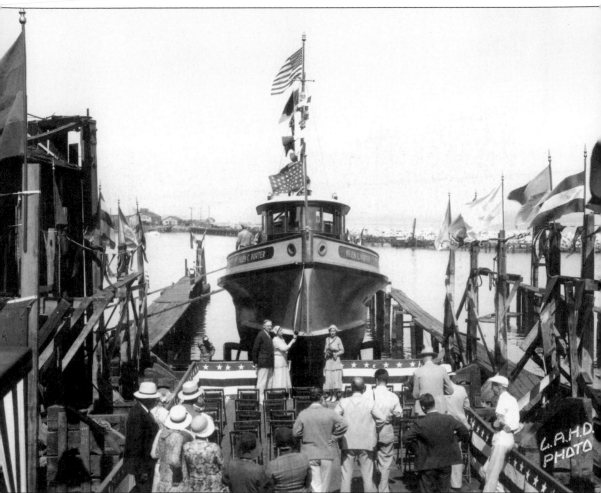

AL LARSON BOAT SHOP, 1931. The wife of Los Angeles mayor John Clinton Porter poses for a photograph before officially launching the pilot boat *Helen C. Porter*, named in her honor, down the ways of the Al Larson Boat Shop. At the same location near Berth 224 since 1903, the boatyard is the oldest continuously operating business at the port. The yard was established on Terminal Island on the Main Channel by Swedish immigrant Peter "Al" Larson, who settled in San Pedro after working for several years at a shipyard in San Francisco. (Courtesy of the Port of Los Angeles Archive.)

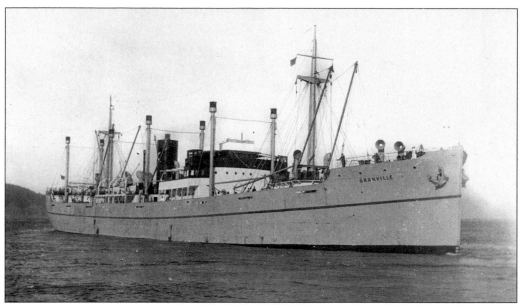

NEW TRANSPACIFIC SERVICE, 1932. Norway's Klaveness Line began scheduled service from the port to the Orient with the Port of Kobe, Japan, as the first port-of-call. The first ship to sail on the new route was the refrigerator ship *Granville*, which sailed from the port on March 9 for Kobe, Shanghai, Singapore, Batavia, and other Dutch East Indies ports. (Courtesy of the Allan Knight Collection, Monterey Maritime and History Museum.)

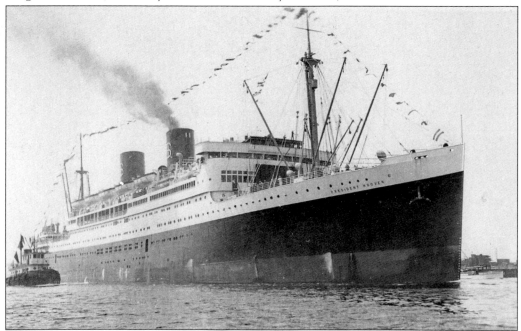

PRESIDENT HOOVER, 1932. The Dollar Steamship Company—predecessor to American President Lines—operated the liner *President Hoover* on a regular service between California and ports in the Far East. The liner came to grief in 1937 when she went aground on Hoishoto Island off the southern coast of Taiwan. She was declared a total loss and broken up for scrap where she lay. (Author's collection.)

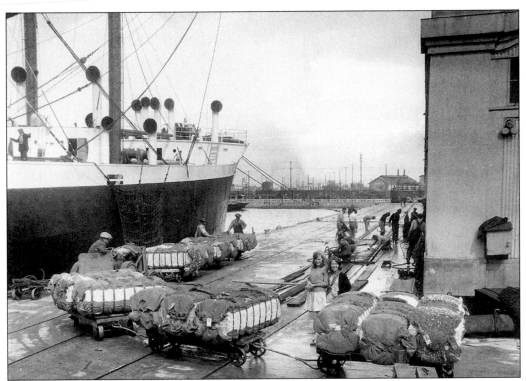

CALIFORNIA COTTON, 1932. Two young ladies enjoy the show as they watch a shipment of California-grown cotton being loaded aboard a waiting freighter for shipment to European textile mills. That year, the port handled 126,000 bales of cotton, more than any other West Coast port. (Courtesy of the Port of Los Angeles Archive.)

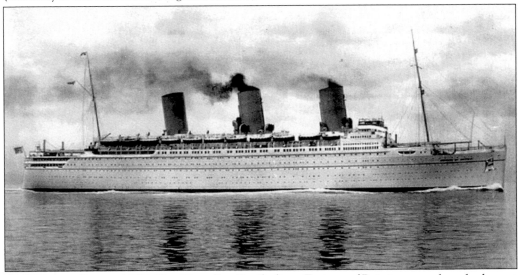

AN EMPRESS CALLS, 1932. The Canadian Pacific liner *Empress of Britain* was to date the largest merchant vessel of any kind to ever call at the Port of Los Angeles. She dropped anchor in the roadstead in March. The 63,000-ton ship was flagship of the Canadian Pacific fleet and was on the last lap of her first round-the-world voyage, which had started in New York the previous December. (Author's collection.)

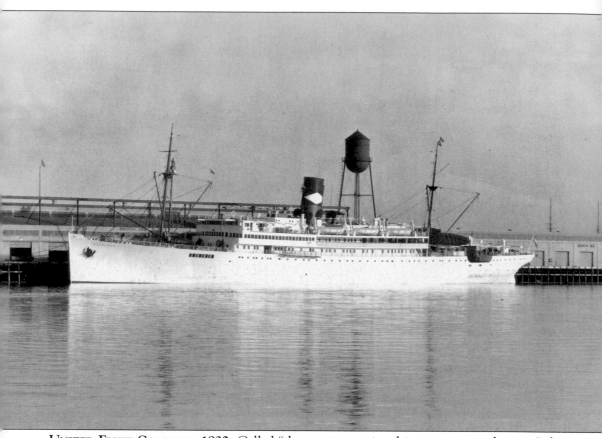

UNITED FRUIT COMPANY, 1932. Called "the most attractive ship to ever visit the port," the gleaming *Talamanca* made her maiden arrival at the Port of Los Angeles in January. The ship docked at Berth 188 in Wilmington with 100 passengers and 45,000 stems of Grade 9 bananas, 19,000 of which were discharged at the company's facility. (Author's collection.)

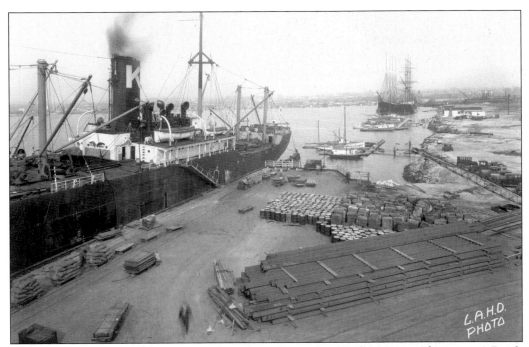

OUTBOUND FOR THE ORIENT, 1932. The "K" Line steamer *Wales Maru* works cargo at Berth 230-E in the East Basin. Ahead of her are calls at Yokohama, Kobe, Osaka, and Shanghai via San Francisco. Baled cargo and barrels wait on the dock, while two idled sailing ships sit in the background at their final berth. (Courtesy of the Port of Los Angeles Archive.)

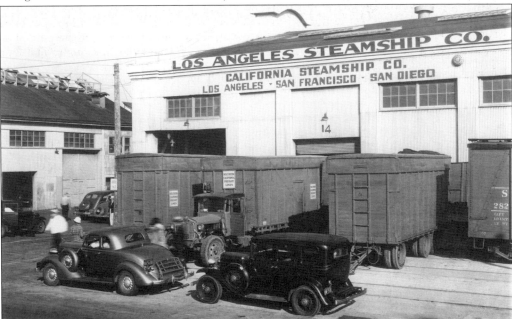

TRUCK LINES, 1932. A Southern California Freight Lines truck awaits loading and two vans await unloading at the Los Angeles Steamship Company warehouse. By the 1930s, trucks were offering door-to-door service for more than 65 percent of the cargo moving through the port to and from points in California, from San Francisco to San Diego. (Courtesy of the Sherman Library.)

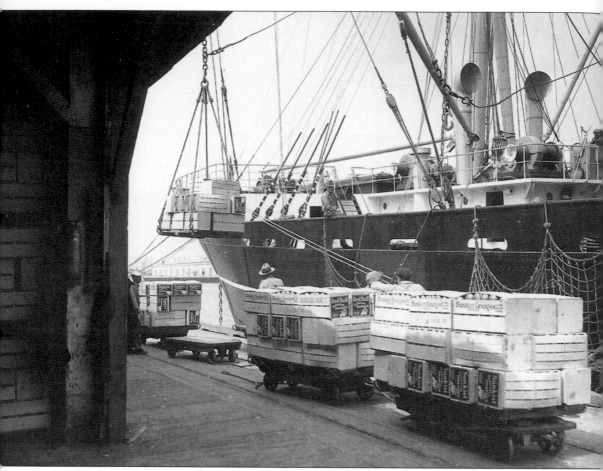

OUTBOUND CITRUS, 1932. Sunkist oranges are loaded aboard an unidentified freighter for shipment to overseas markets. Sunkist Growers was previously known as the California Fruit Growers Exchange; it served as a cooperative for more than 20,000 growers in California and Arizona that supplied the five million crates of oranges, lemons, and grapefruit exported through the port during that year alone. (Courtesy of the Sherman Library.)

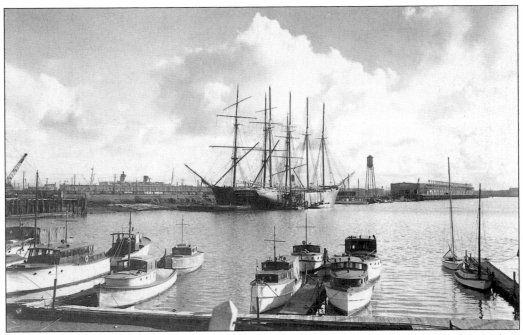

EAST BASIN, 1932. The heyday of commercial sailing ships had long passed when these sailing ships tied up to their last berth in the port's East Basin. Many spent their last days as barges, while others were sunk far offshore or simply left to rot away at their final berths. (Courtesy of the Sherman Library.)

AN UNUSUAL LIFT, 1935. In one of the most unusual shipments ever handled at the harbor, a crowd of interested longshoremen watches as a circus elephant is calmly sling-loaded onto a freighter with a specially built pen on its foredeck. In the years to come, the harbor would see everything from farm equipment and school buses to armored cars and bulldozers cross its docks. (Courtesy of the Sherman Library.)

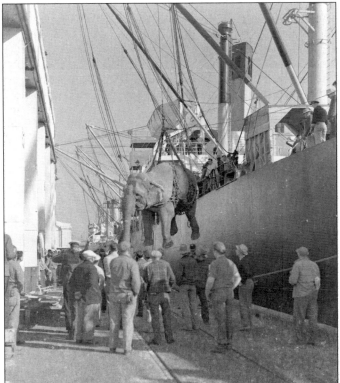

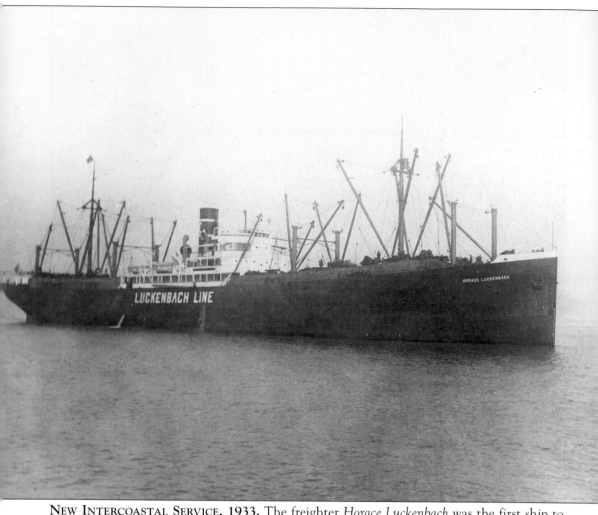

NEW INTERCOASTAL SERVICE, 1933. The freighter *Horace Luckenbach* was the first ship to call at the Port of Los Angeles, inaugurating the Luckenbach Steamship Company's new intercoastal service in April. (Courtesy of the Allen Knight Collection, Monterey Maritime and History Museum.)

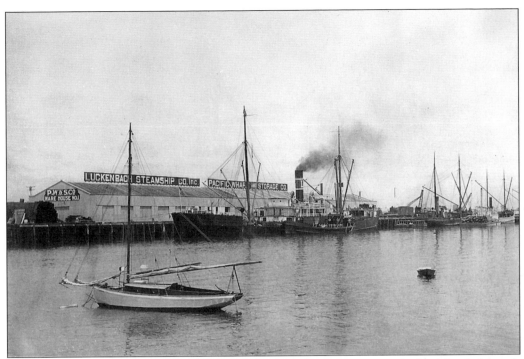

LUCKENBACK LINE, 1933. An unidentified Luckenback freighter is seen at the line's berth (above). The warehouse at the berth was operated by the Pacific Warehouse and Storage Company. The 14,221-ton freighter *Louis Luckenbach* (below) was the largest ship operated by the line on the route linking the U.S. West and East Coasts via the Panama Canal. (Above, courtesy of the Port of Los Angeles Archives; below, courtesy of the Allen Knight Collection, Monterey Maritime and History Museum.)

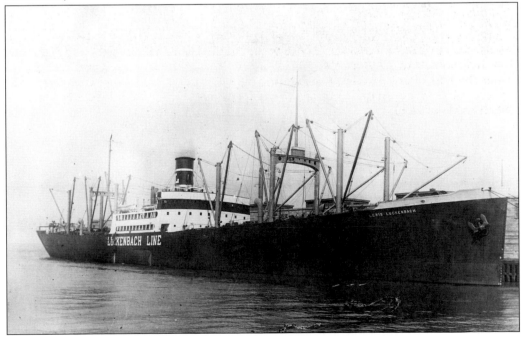

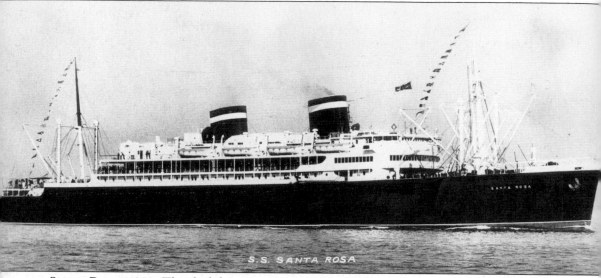

S.S. SANTA ROSA

SANTA ROSA, 1932. The sleek liner *Santa Rosa* was the first of four passenger ships that Grace Line operated on the route linking Los Angeles and San Francisco with Central America, Cuba, and New York via the Panama Canal. (Courtesy of the Allen Knight Collection, Monterey Maritime and History Museum.)

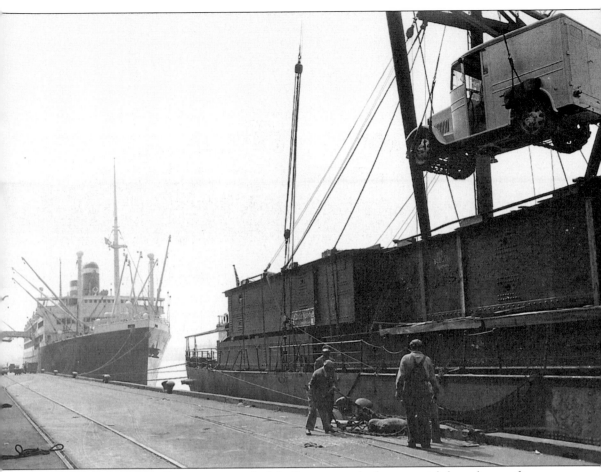

BARGE CARGO, 1933. Barges carrying fuel, bulk cargo, and other materials have been a fixture at the Port of Los Angeles since its earliest days. This image shows a milk truck lifted onto a barge for shipment to a dairy in San Francisco. (Courtesy of the Port of Los Angeles Archive.)

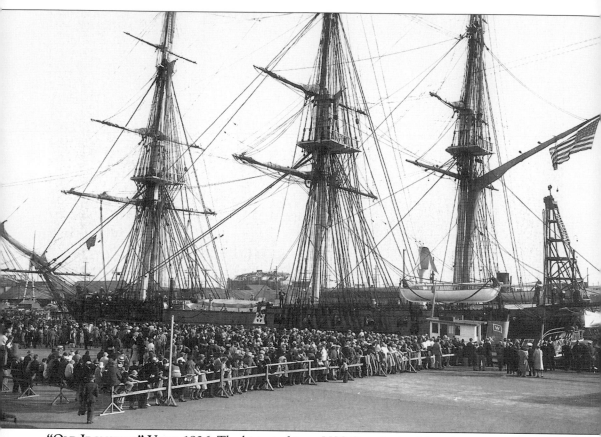

"Old Ironsides" Visit, 1936. The historic frigate USS *Constitution* (above) was visited by more than 500,000 Southern Californians when she made a historic call at the Port of Los Angeles during a months-long tour of ports along the East Coast, Gulf of Mexico, and West Coast. (Courtesy of the Sherman Library.)

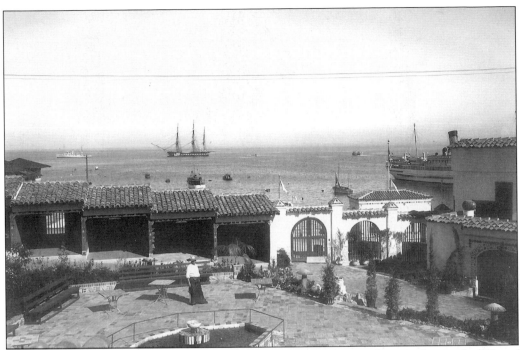

USS Constitution, 1936. "Old Ironsides"—which earned it's nickname during the War of 1812—can be seen (above) at anchor shortly after she arrived at the port. Astern of a U.S. Navy tug (below), she was later docked at Berth 57. (Both courtesy of the Title Insurance Trust Collection, University of Southern California.)

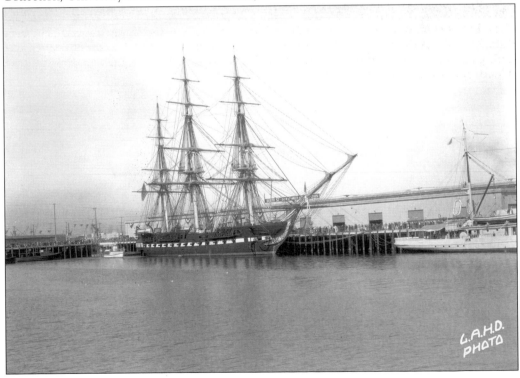

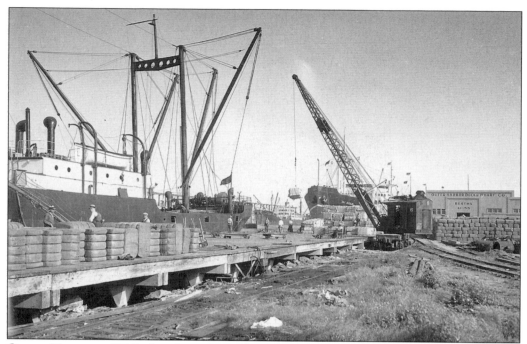

OUTER HARBOR, 1936. A railcar-mounted steam crane stacks baled cotton wharf-side as an unidentified freighter waits for her cargo at Berth 41–55 in the port's Outer Harbor. Flying the Blue Peter, signaling she's about to sail, the Norwegian-flag *Tai Shan* is berthed astern with an export cargo for Shanghai and Hong Kong. (Courtesy of the Sherman Library.)

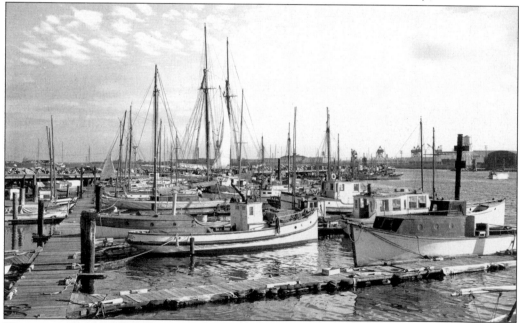

WATCHORN BASIN, 1937. Named for Union Oil executive and philanthropist Robert Watchorn, the basin covers Berths 40–44 and originally was the site of a U.S. Navy fuel dock. Over the years, it was transformed into the port's yacht anchorage and is now part of Cabrillo Beach near the port's West Channel. (Courtesy of the Port of Los Angeles Archive.)

UNLOADING STEEL, 1937. Steel pipe is unloaded from the freighter *Pacific* onto gondola cars waiting on the cluttered wharf. For the first time since the start of the Great Depression seven years earlier, the volume of import and export cargo moving through the port passed 20 million tons. (Courtesy of the Port of Los Angeles Archive.)

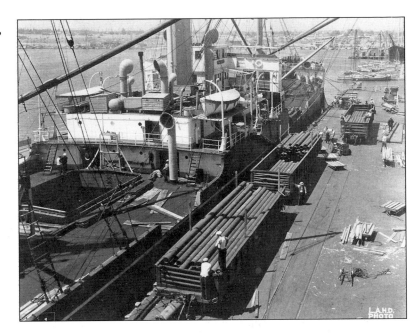

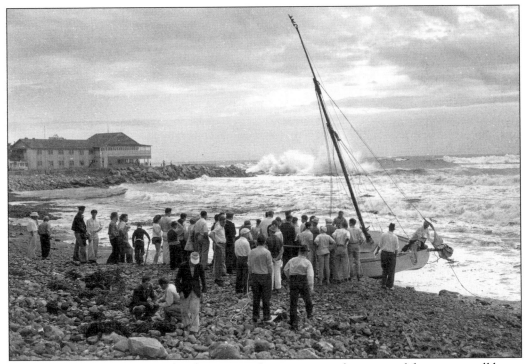

BOAT ASHORE, 1939. A crowd gathers to watch attempts to salvage one of the many small boats driven ashore after a five-day storm that slammed into the Southern California coastline. The storm was one of the worst in memory, repeatedly smashing into the Angel's Gate Light and giving it a slight tilt that it has to this day. (Courtesy of the Newport Beach Nautical Museum.)

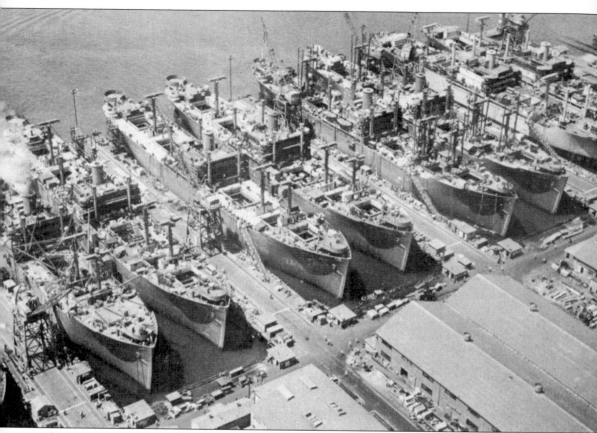

CALSHIP, 1940. California Shipbuilding Corporation was built on a patch of mudflats on Terminal Island in the months prior to America's involvement in World War II. The yard was the third "emergency shipyard" built on the West Coast and boasted 14 launching ways. By the end of the war, the yard had produced 467 oil tankers and Liberty, Victory, and maritime-classified freighters at an average cost of $1,858,000 each. (Courtesy of the California State University, Northridge Special Collection.)

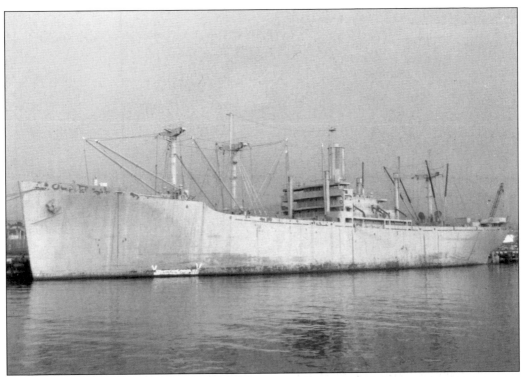

VICTORY SHIPS, 1940. The *Lane Victory* (above) was delivered by Calship in June 1945. The ship is now a floating museum and is berthed in the shadow of the Vincent Thomas Bridge, just a short distance from where she was launched more than 60 years earlier. Just 19 months after her launch in June 1944, the Calship-built *Luray Victory* (below) went aground on the treacherous Goodwin Sands reef off the southwest coast of England and was pounded to pieces. (Both author's collection.)

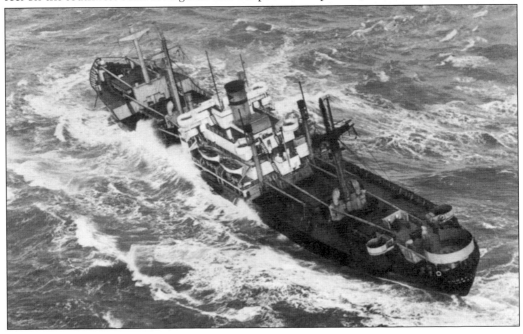

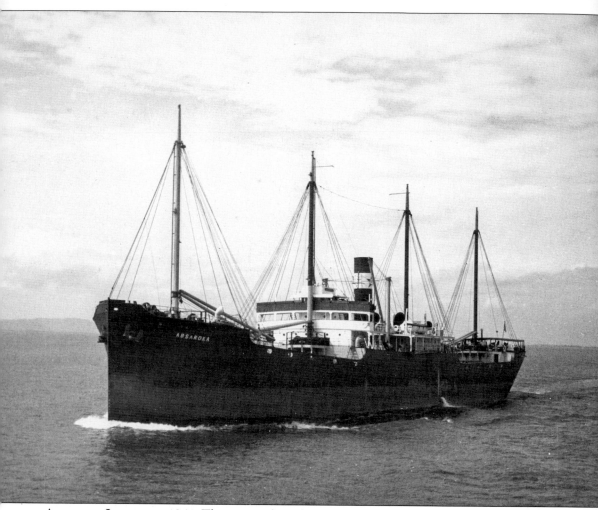

ABSAROKA INCIDENT, 1941. The grim reality of war arrived at the port on Christmas Eve, 1941, when the 5,700-ton freighter *Absaroka* was torpedoed by the Japanese submarine I-19 about 25 miles off Point Fermin Lighthouse. The unarmed McCormack Line ship was bound for Los Angeles with a cargo of Pacific Northwest lumber, which was credited with keeping her afloat after she was hit. The ship was abandoned after the torpedoing but was later reboarded and towed into San Pedro, where she was repaired. One of the ship's 33 crewmen was killed in the attack. (Courtesy of the Allan Knight Collection, Monterey Maritime and History Museum.)

Four

THE POSTWAR BOOM

When the U.S. Navy officially relinquished its wartime control of the Port of Los Angeles in late 1945, the door opened to a period of unprecedented growth for both the Port of Los Angeles and Southern California.

The end of the war saw hundreds of thousands of former servicemen and their families move into the region, swelling the population and exponentially increasing its economic vitality. With a domino-like effect, more people meant more business and more business meant more trade and more trade meant more cargo moving back and forth across the port's docks.

Granted a Foreign Trade Zone charter in 1949, the port enhanced its cargo-handling capability over the following decade with several steamship lines, including American President Lines and Matson Navigation Company, constructing new cargo and passenger terminals. With an eye toward marketing its capabilities globally, the port opened the doors at its first trade development office in Oslo, Norway, with a second a few months later in Tokyo, Japan.

The significance of the Tokyo office was underscored by the growth in the volume of trade between the United States and Japan that was moving through the port. Full-scale maritime trade with Japan, restricted since 1941, was resumed a decade later, and within five years, Japanese-flag ships topped the list of calls at the port with 324.

By the late 1950s, export cargo moving through the Port of Los Angeles was headed to 114 overseas markets with almost two-thirds going to points along the Pacific Rim.

Despite the dominance of the transpacific trades in the port's growth, however, trade with Europe continued to play a significant role in its operations with several steamship lines such as the East Asiatic Company, Maersk, and the Johnson Line offering all-water routings to Northern Europe and Mediterranean ports.

But as the opening of the distant Panama Canal opened new trade routes that revitalized the life of the port, a not-so-new shipping technology—containerization—would, quite literally, revolutionize and transform the way both the world and the Port of Los Angeles did business.

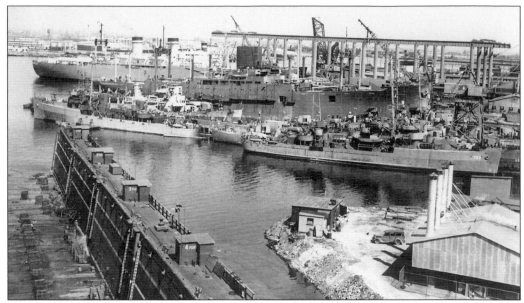

POSTWAR STAND-DOWN, 1946. The end of World War II found hundreds of U.S. Navy ships needing to be surveyed for disposition, whether that meant lay-up in reserve for future use, prepared for transfer to the navies of other countries, or scrapped, while others were upgraded for retention on active duty. Todd Shipyard in San Pedro was tasked with a significant amount of that government work. Several ships including a minesweeper, a pair of troop transports, and a pair of destroyer escorts can be seen above, while below one of the yards' several cranes looms over many ships with an empty dry dock in the background. (Both courtesy of the California State University Northridge Library Special Collection.)

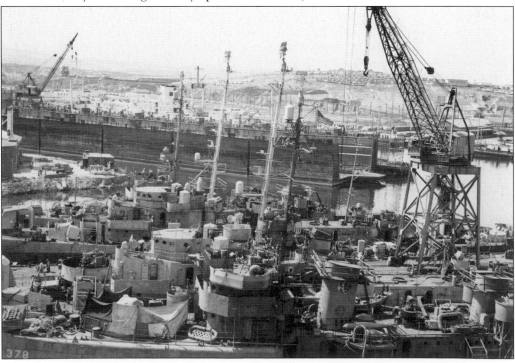

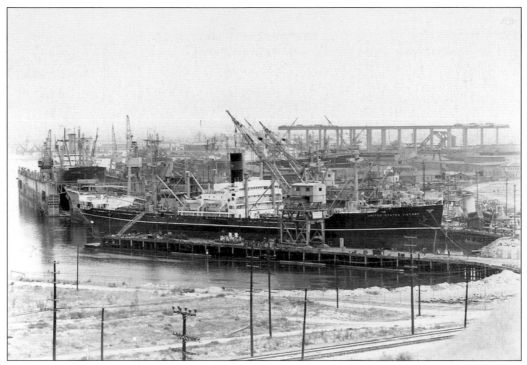

REPAIR WORK, 1947. The *United States Victory* was built at the California Shipbuilding yard in San Pedro in 1944. The ship visited the Todd Shipyard three years later for an engine overhaul just a few months before she was sold to foreign interests. (Author's collection.)

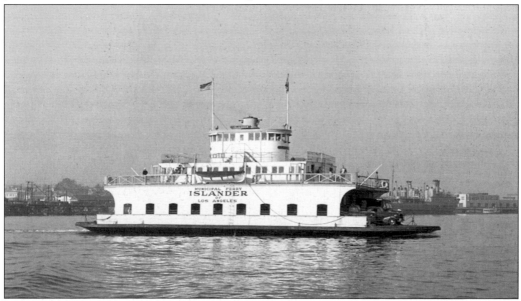

TERMINAL ISLAND FERRY, 1948. The *Islander* served as the only public access between "mainland" San Pedro and Terminal Island from 1941 to 1963, when the four-lane Vincent Thomas Bridge, built over three years at a cost of more than $21 million, was dedicated. The ferry can be seen crossing the port's Main Channel on her 10-minute "voyage" with a pair of tankers berthed in the background. (Author's collection.)

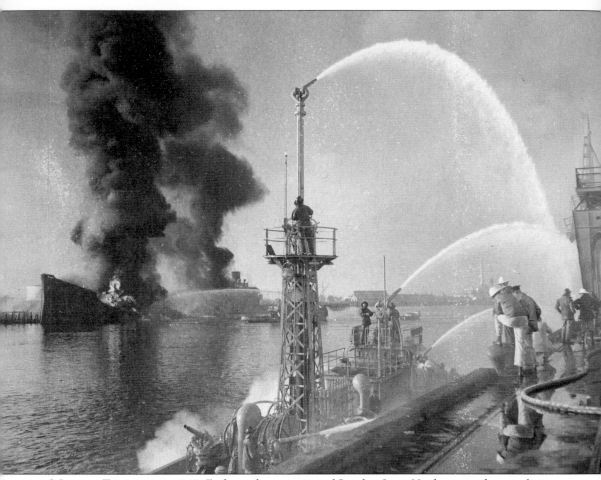

MARKAY EXPLOSION, 1947. Early in the morning of Sunday, June 22, the second-worst disaster to strike the port to date occurred when the tanker *Markay* exploded at the Shell Oil Company wharf. The blast killed 11 people and injured 23 others as flames crossed the oil-covered channel and destroyed most of the American President Lines cargo terminal at Berths 153–155. (Courtesy of the Los Angeles Fire Department Museum.)

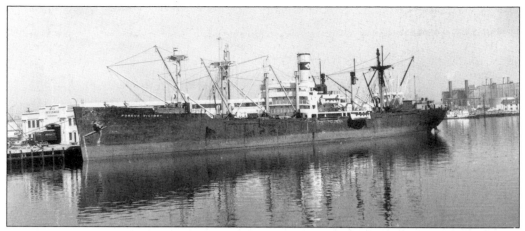

PURDUE VICTORY, 1949. The postwar years saw many ships that had been built to carry supplies and troops during the conflict sold to private steamship lines for use on cargo routes around the world. The *Purdue Victory* sailed for the Waterman Steamship Company on the company's route linking the U.S. Gulf Coast with the Orient. The ship was an occasional visitor to the port's facilities at Berths 176–178. (Author's collection.)

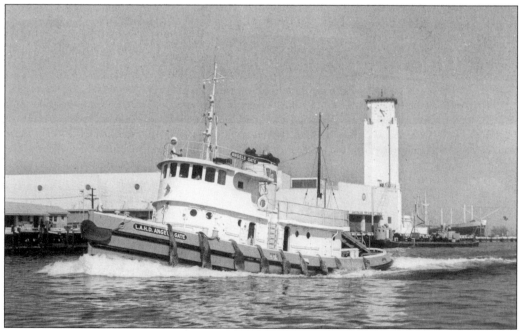

CITY TUG, 1949. The tug *Angel's Gate* served at the port towing derrick and fuel barges and transporting pilots to waiting ships for the Los Angeles Harbor Department until her retirement in 1992. The craft was built for the U.S. Army in 1944 for use in European waters. (Author's collection.)

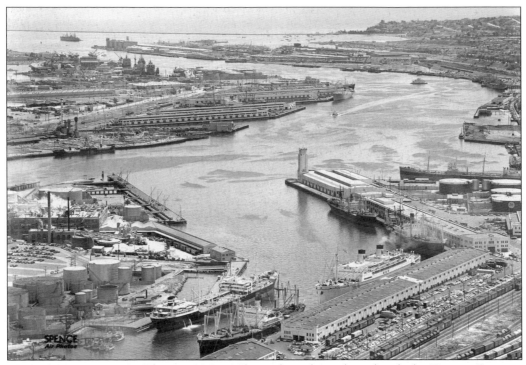

MAIN CHANNEL, 1953. The port's Main Channel winds southward with the Turning Basin to the right and Warehouse No. 1 in the distance. Several ships can be seen in the foreground, while the Terminal Island ferry can be seen in mid-channel. (Author's collection.)

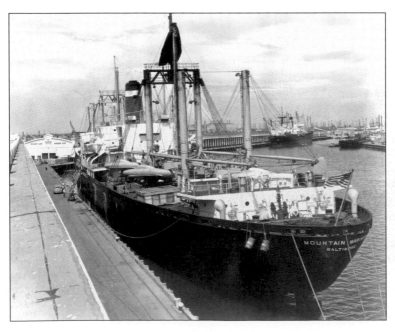

DECK CARGO FOR KOREA, 1953. The *Mountain Mariner* is seen at Berths 153–155 near the junction of the Turning Basin and the port's East Channel. The ship carries a deck load of U.S. Air Force F-84 Thunderjets for shipment to the Korean battlefront. The aircraft have been waterproofed to prevent corrosion from the elements during the ship's 12-day transit to the combat zone. (Author's collection.)

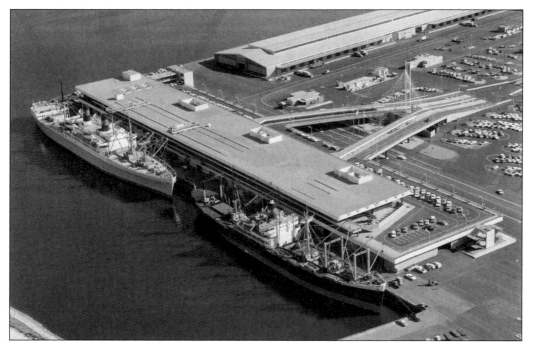

AMERICAN PRESIDENT LINES TERMINAL, 1953. San Francisco–headquartered American President Lines began construction at Berth 154 on its first combination passenger/cargo terminal at the Port of Los Angeles in 1950. The passenger liner *President Cleveland* is seen (left) berthed at the terminal with the C-3 cargo/passenger liner *President McKinley*. (Author's collection.)

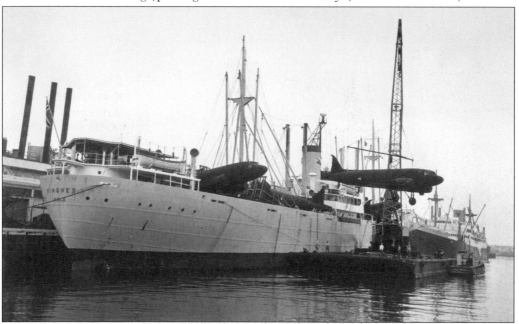

EXPORT AIRCRAFT, 1954. A pair of war-surplus DC-3 transport planes was loaded onto the aft deck of the Norwegian freighter *Vignes* for shipment to the Baltic. The Douglas-built passenger-cargo aircraft were refurbished for use by SAS Airlines at the company's aircraft production facility in nearby El Segundo. (Author's collection.)

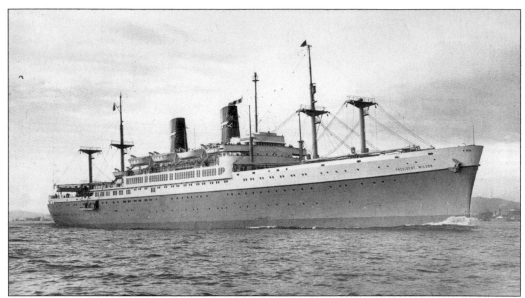

PRESIDENT WILSON, 1954. Ships that sail for American President Lines and its predecessor, the Dollar Steamship Company, have called at the port since the 1920s. One of the most beautiful was the passenger liner *President Wilson*. Built in 1948, the ship could accommodate 550 first- and "economy"-class passengers on the company's route between California and the Far East and was highly regarded by all who sailed aboard her. (Author's collection.)

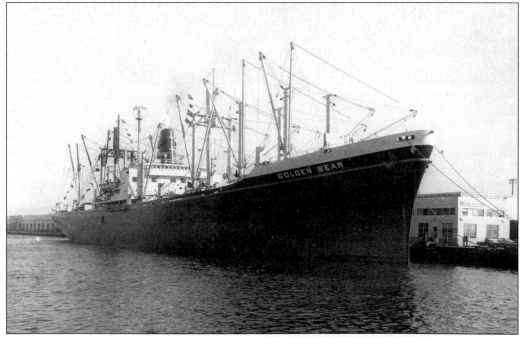

GOLDEN BEAR, 1955. The Mariner class of ships was designed as modernized replacements for the war-weary freighters that made up a large part of the postwar U.S. merchant fleet. The 546-foot, 22,500-ton *Golden Bear* was one of the first of the Mariners and was operated by Pacific Far East Line. She called at the Port of Los Angeles on its regular route between California and ports throughout the Far East. (Author's collection.)

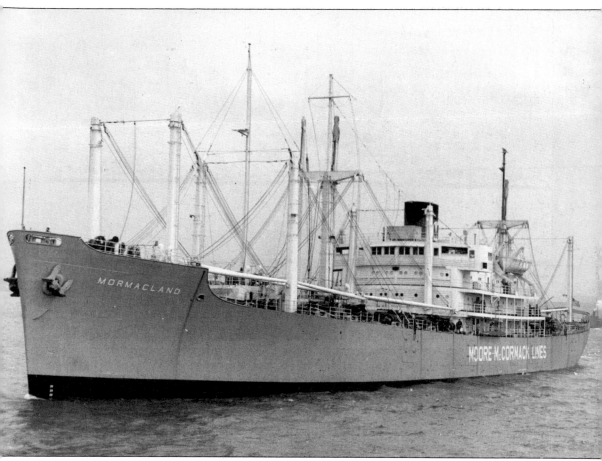

LATIN AMERICAN ROUTE, 1956. Known for years in the lucrative U.S.–South American trades, Moore-McCormack Lines operated the *Mormacland* and five other ships in a service between U.S. West Coast ports, Central America, and the east coast of South America. The ship had substantial space for refrigerated cargo and could carry 12 passengers. When at the port, the ship tied up at Berth 232-A in Wilmington. Moore-McCormack ceased operations in 1982 after 61 years in the maritime trades. (Author's collection.)

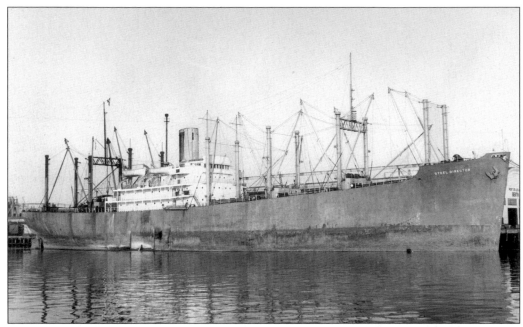

ISTHMIAN LINES, 1956. The U.S.-flag *Steel Director* sailed on a biweekly service between the Port of Los Angeles and Manila, Saigon, Bangkok, Singapore, and other Southeast Asian ports. A subsidiary of the U.S. Steel company, Isthmian Lines operated 85 ships during the postwar years but was absorbed by rival States Marine Lines when U.S. Steel decided it was more cost-efficient to outsource its shipping operations. (Author's collection.)

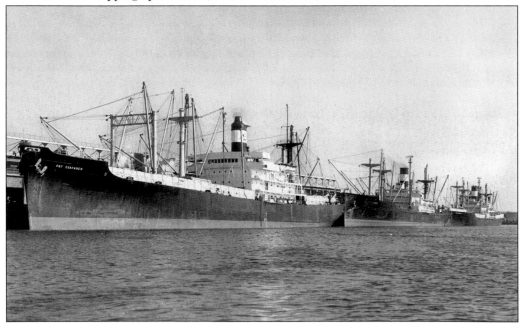

POPE AND TALBOT, 1956. With a deck load of lumber, the *P&T Seafarer* and a pair of sister ships sit at Berth 146 in Wilmington. The three freighters sailed on the route connecting ports on the U.S. West Coast and the north and east coasts of South America via the Panama Canal. (Author's collection.)

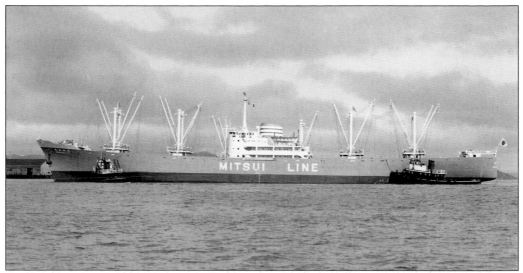

JAPAN TRADE SURGE, 1957. In 1957, Japanese-flag ships topped the list of ship calls at the port with more than 350. The green-hulled Mitsui Line cargo liner *Mayasan Maru*, pictured here, is assisted by a tug on her way up the Main Channel to tie up at Berth 145 in Wilmington. (Author's collection.)

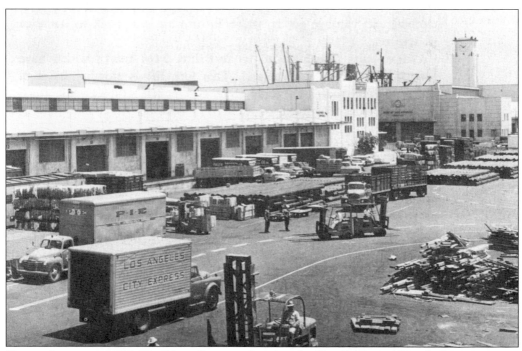

TRUCK ACTIVITY, 1957. On a busy afternoon, Los Angeles City Express and Pacific Intermountain Express trucks move freight on the land side of the warehouse at Berths 153–155. As in earlier years, trucks continued to move a majority of the cargo between the port and points throughout California and the greater metropolitan Los Angeles area. (Courtesy of the Port of Los Angeles Archive.)

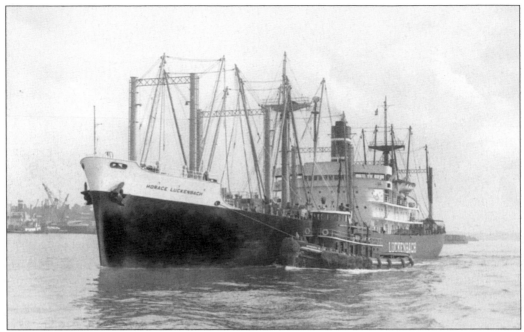

LUCKENBACH LINE, 1957. The Luckenbach Steamship Company inaugurated intercoastal service between the East Coast, the Gulf of Mexico, and the West Coast in the 1930s. The *Horace Luckenbach*, the second ship to bear that name, was one of the C-3-type cargo ships operated in the postwar years on the company's weekly service via the Panama Canal and other routes. (Author's collection.)

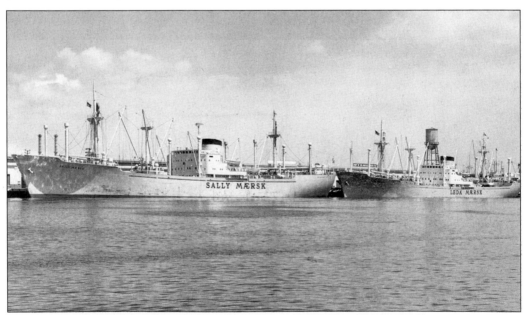

MAERSK, 1957. A pair of Danish-flag Maersk Line ships awaits export cargo at Berth 158 in Wilmington. With their signature powder-blue hulls, Maersk Line ships had been calling at the port since the late 1920s. In the decades to follow, the Copenhagen-headquartered company would evolve into one of the world's largest steamship companies. (Author's collection.)

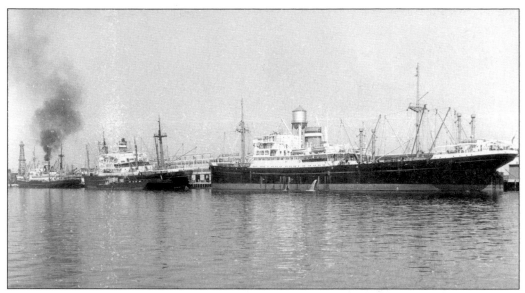

European Trade Routes, 1957. In April, three Dutch-flag Holland-America Line freighters—the *Diemerdyk*, the *Dinteldyk*, and the *Moerdyk*—had their calls at the port overlap (above). The three ships and another sister operated on the line's Northern Europe–U.S. West Coast route through the 1950s. (Author's collection.)

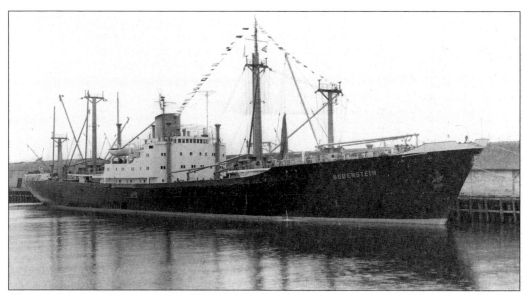

North German Lloyd, 1958. North German Lloyd's *Bodenstein* was a regular at the port, competing with Holland America and a dozen other steamship lines including the Fred Olsen Line of Sweden and Italy's Italnavi Line. North German Lloyd operated its service in cooperation with Hapag Lloyd, Germany's largest steamship company. (Author's collection.)

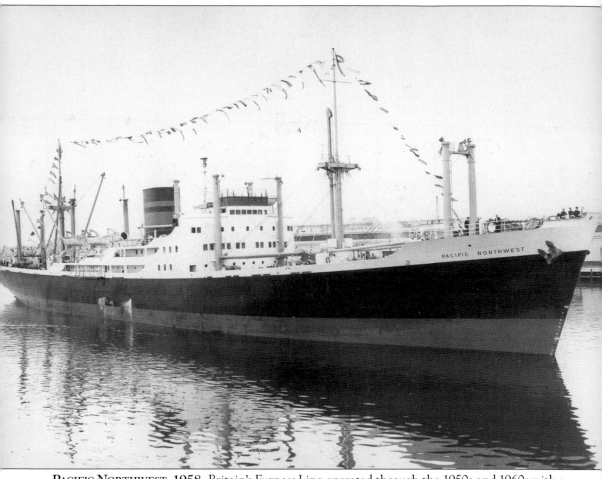

PACIFIC NORTHWEST, 1958. Britain's Furness Line operated through the 1950s and 1960s with a three-ship service connecting London, Liverpool, and Manchester with Seattle, San Francisco, and Los Angeles, where the motor ship *Pacific Northwest* loaded and discharged cargo in Wilmington at Berths 188–191. (Author's collection.)

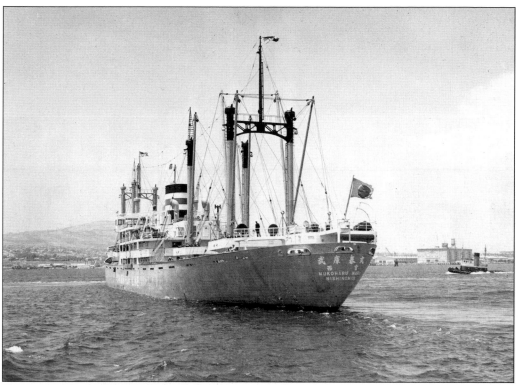

SHINNIHON LINE, 1958. The *Mukoharu Maru* (above) turns into the port's Main Channel with a cargo of consumer products for discharge. Warehouse No. 1 is seen in the distance. A sister ship, the *Hiyeharu Maru* (below), glides through the breakwater after calls at Yokohama, Kobe, Nagoya, and Osaka. (Both author's collection.)

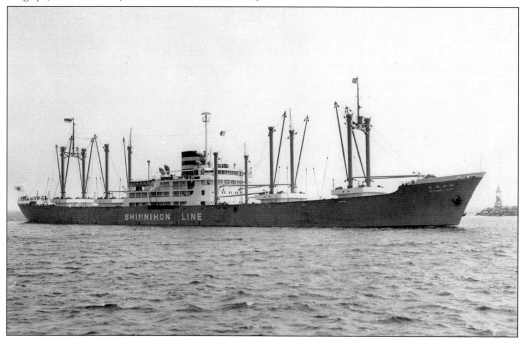

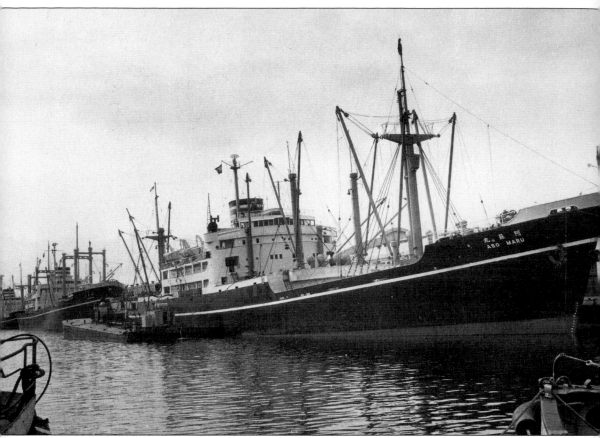

NIPPON YUSEN KAISHA, 1958. Sporting Nippon Yusen Kaisha's distinctive double red band–on–white funnel markings, the *Aso Maru* awaits an export cargo for Japan and the Far East. The company, known universally as NYK, emerged from World War II with only 37 ships, but in the following decades rebuilt itself into Japan's largest steamship line with one of the largest fleets of containerships, bulk and automobile carriers, and tankers in the world. (Author's collection.)

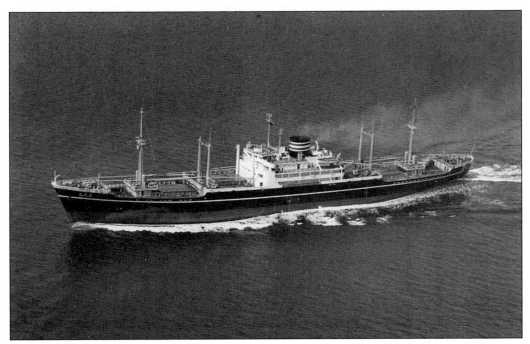

NYK, 1958. The *Asama Maru* (above) heads north to San Francisco after clearing Angel's Gate to call at San Francisco, while the *Shimane Maru* (below) is seen at Berth 158 in Wilmington celebrating her maiden arrival at the Port of Los Angeles. Separate NYK routes linked the port with Kobe, Nagoya, Yokohama, Northern Europe, and the west coast of South America. (Both author's collection.)

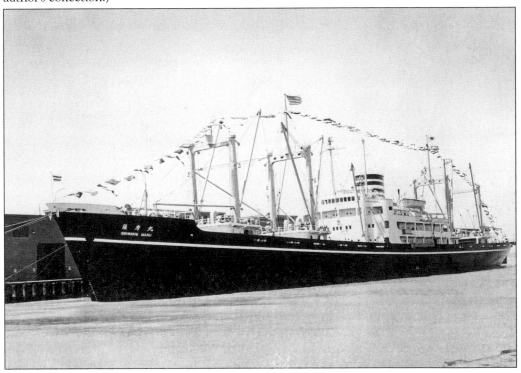

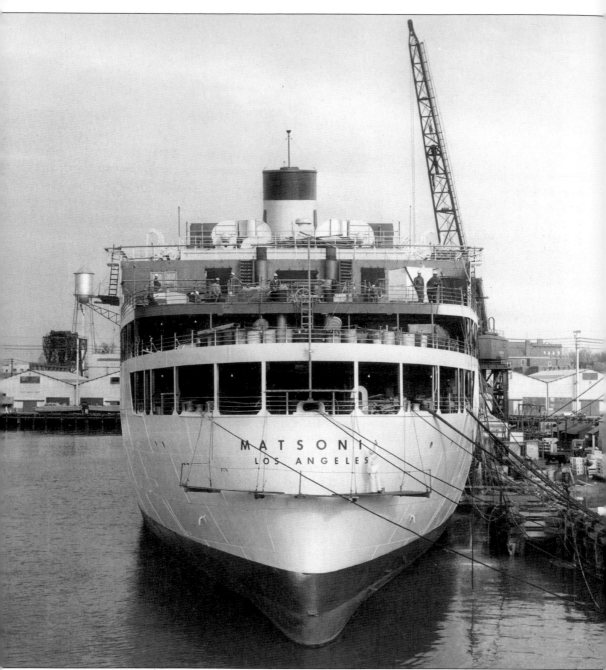

MATSONIA, 1957. Launched as the *Monterey* in 1932 for the Oceanic Steamship Company, the white-hulled *Matsonia* later sailed for the Matson Navigation Company. The liner was rechristened with her new name and arrived in Los Angeles on her maiden voyage in May 1957. She linked the port with Honolulu under her second name until she was renamed once more, this time as the *Lurline* in 1963. (Author's collection.)

Five

THE PORT AND THE MAGIC BOX

While the bragging rights as to who actually "invented" containerization will be up for grabs for generations to come, there can be no doubt about the sweeping, revolutionary impact the technology has had on the world's economic geography.

By the 1960s, the Port of Los Angeles had firmly established itself as a world-class port with its bustling operations fueled not only by local and regional business needs, but, increasingly, by the growing volume of cargo moving through the port to and from points across the country.

The transformation put the port at the very cutting edge of developing terminals and infrastructure to handle the flow of containerized cargo that would, over the years, grow into a deluge.

The Matson Navigation Company pioneered containerization at the port in the late 1950s, and by 1960, its relatively primitive box terminals had handled a mere 7,000 containers. Only nine years later, however, that figure had grown tenfold—in no small part because the port began operating as the U.S. port of call for the very first container service linking Japan and the United States in 1968.

Over the last several decades, the ongoing development of rail facilities—both on-dock and in close proximity to the port—has significantly improved the handling of both inbound and outbound containers moving between Southern California and business centers throughout the United States. The construction of these rail terminals has become a key component of the Port of Los Angeles's Master Development Plan, while the deepening of the harbor to accommodate future generations of mega-containerships is also a priority.

Now the country's busiest container port and the eighth busiest in the world, the Port of Los Angeles saw 8.5 million boxes move through its terminals in 2006 with one forecast stating that the port could handle as many as 20 million containers annually by 2020.

The last century has seen the Port of Los Angeles develop from a mere "harbor" into one of the world's premier revolving doors for international trade. Driven by both regional and global economic growth, the port has weathered political infighting, war, economic downturns, and other challenges to rightfully claim the title of "WorldPort L.A."

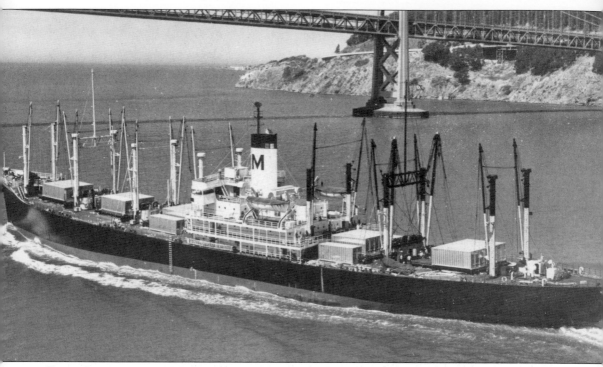

FIRST CONTAINERS, 1958. In August 1958, the Matson Navigation freighter *Hawaiian Merchant*, seen heading out of San Francisco Bay, sailed from a temporary container wharf at Berth 135 with 20 aluminum containers bound for Honolulu, Hawaii—the first container shipment handled at the Port of Los Angeles. The event proved to be one of the most significant in the entire history of the port. (Courtesy of the Matson Navigation Company Archive.)

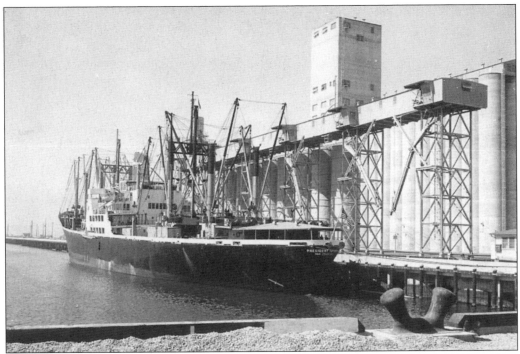

AMERICAN PRESIDENT LINES, 1960. Successor to the Dollar Steamship Line, American President Lines (APL) ships have called at the port for more than 75 years. The *President Taylor*, pictured here, waits to load a cargo at one of the port's bulk terminals. (Author's collection.)

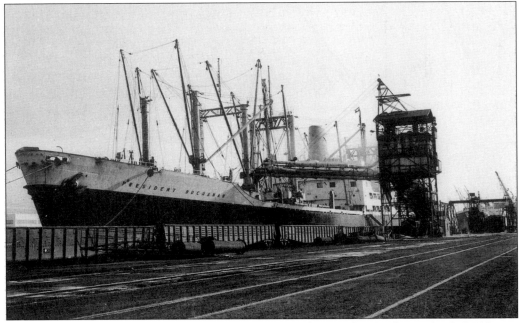

POTASH FOR EXPORT, 1960. Another APL cargo liner, the *President Buchanan*, loads 5,000 tons of bulk potash for shipment to Japan. As in the 1920s, potash continued to be a major export commodity at the port through the decade. The potash was used in the manufacture of glass and ceramics, as well as in the production of soap and fertilizer. (Author's collection.)

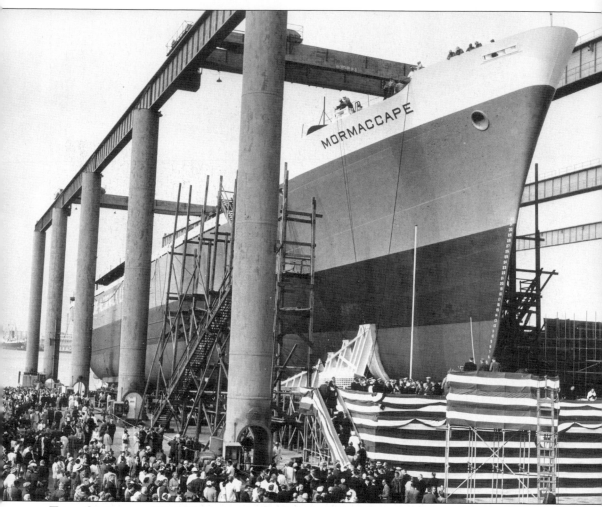

Todd Shipyard, 1960. Guests await the launch of the Moore-McCormack Lines cargo liner *Mormaccape*. The 483-foot ship, known during construction as Hull No. 74, featured one of the first fully automated engine rooms and had accommodations for 12 passengers. The Todd Los Angeles Division in San Pedro also completed a rather unconventional project for the Walt Disney Company—the construction of the stern-wheeler *Mark Twain*, eight 100-ton diesel electric submarines, and the graving dock gates at Disneyland. Todd Los Angeles Division ceased operations in 1989. (Author's collection.)

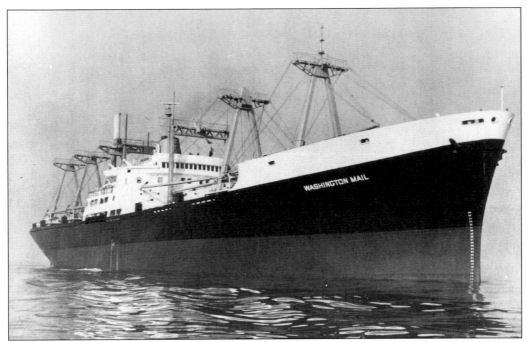

TODD LOS ANGELES DIVISION. The *Washington Mail* (above) was completed for American Mail Line by the Todd Los Angeles Division in 1961 and was converted into a containership 10 years later. The ship later sailed for American President Lines, Delta Lines, and United States Lines before her conversion into a Ready Reserve Force ship for the U.S. Military Sealift Command. Todd also did significant work for the U.S. Navy, including the design and construction of the frigates USS *Wadsworth* and USS *George Philip* (below). (Both author's collection.)

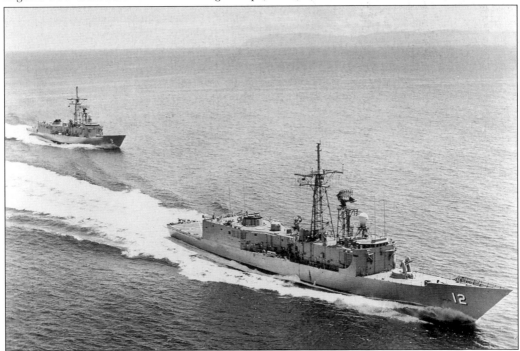

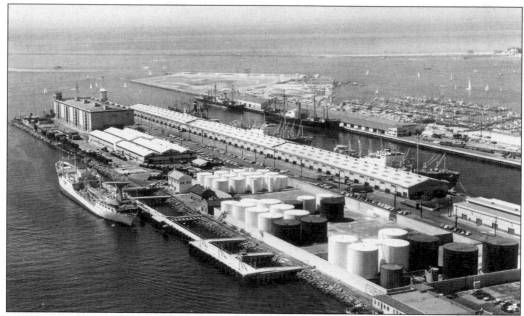

McGuire Terminal, 1961. The tanker *Angelo Petri* is tied up at the company's tank farm on the Main Channel, while five freighters are tied up at Berths 49–55 in the port's East Channel. At the far right is the Watchorn Basin yacht anchorage. The *Angelo Petri* was one of the handful of tankers in the world designed specifically to transport wine. (Author's collection.)

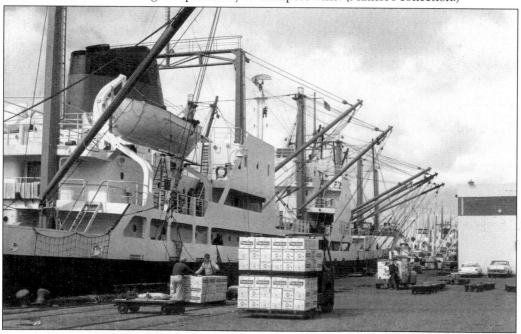

Loading Cargo, 1962. The 1960s saw the maritime industry in the throes of the transition from the more traditional methods of moving cargo to containerization. Despite the shift, though, standard cargo liners carrying import and export cargoes from manufactured goods and steel to bagged and bulk commodities like coffee and cotton continued to keep the port's wharves bustling with activity. (Author's collection.)

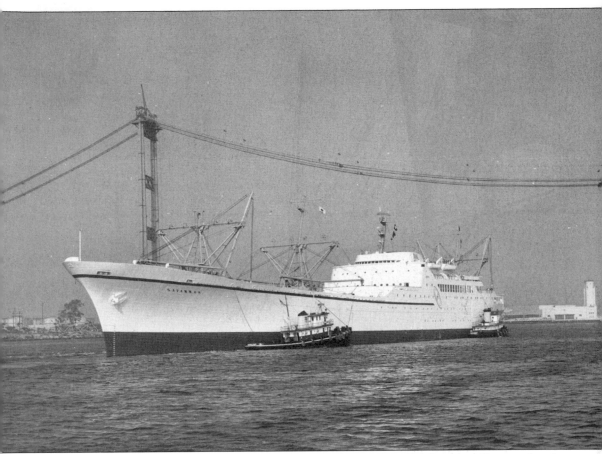

NS *Savannah*, 1962. The nuclear-powered *Savannah* passed under the partially completed Vincent Thomas Bridge with the help of two Wilmington Transportation Company tugboats at the close of a two-day visit to the port. The ship was launched in 1959 and carried 17,000 pounds of enriched uranium that provided enough energy to sail 336,000 miles at 21 knots, or three and a half years of operation, without having to refuel. (Author's collection.)

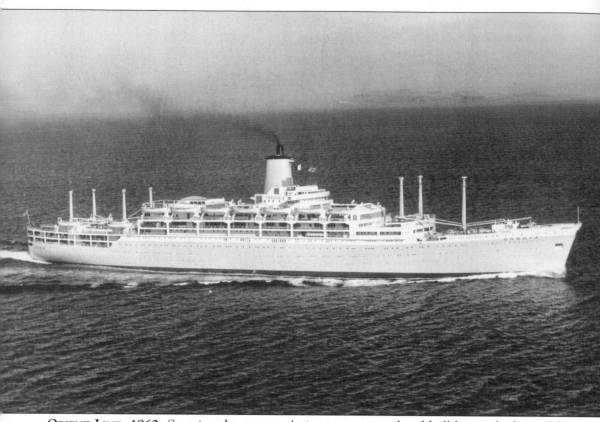

ORIENT LINE, 1962. Sporting the company's signature corn-colored hull livery, the beautiful British-flag *Orsova* was one of a quartet of liners that sailed on the Orient Line's transpacific service. The company operated independently on the route linking Vancouver, San Francisco, and Los Angeles with the Far East and Australia for 10 years before its operations were merged with those of the storied P&O Lines in 1960. (Author's collection.)

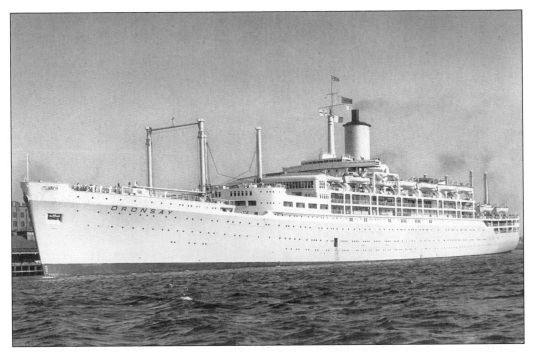

TRANSPACIFIC PASSENGER SERVICE, 1962. The *Oronsay* (above), the *Oriana* (below), and the *Orcades* joined the *Orsova* on the Orient Lines transpacific passenger service. All of the Orient Lines ships used on the transpacific route were built by the British shipbuilding firm of Vickers-Armstrong. (Both author's collection.)

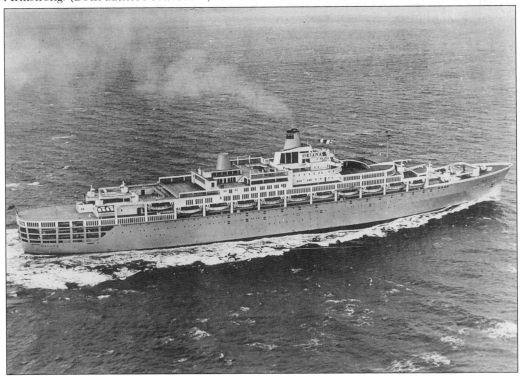

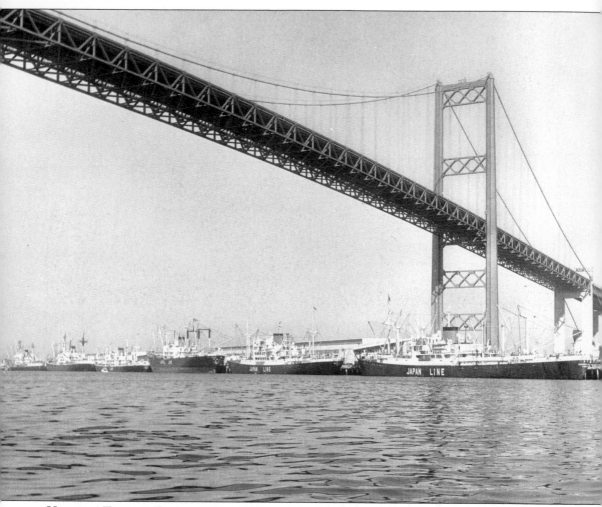

VINCENT THOMAS BRIDGE, 1963. Three years after construction began, the 15,000-foot-long Vincent Thomas Bridge opened to provide a direct link for auto and truck traffic between Terminal Island and San Pedro on the "mainland" side of the port's Main Channel. The suspension bridge is named for the California congressman who led the effort in Washington, D.C., to acquire the $21.4 million in funding needed to build the distinctive, green-painted span. (Author's collection.)

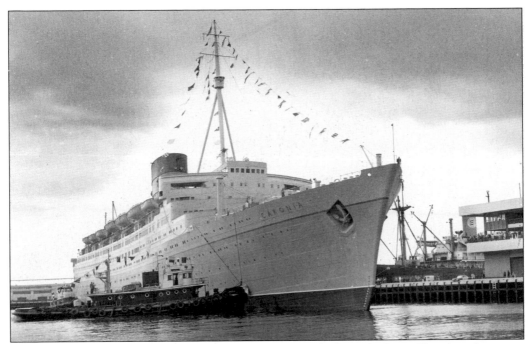

The Caronia Calls, 1964. The Cunard liner *Caronia* docks at the Port of Los Angeles cruise terminal. The terminal had originally been built as a combination passenger-cargo terminal by American President Lines and helped lay the groundwork for the port's current ranking as the busiest cruise and passenger port on the U.S. West Coast. (Author's collection.)

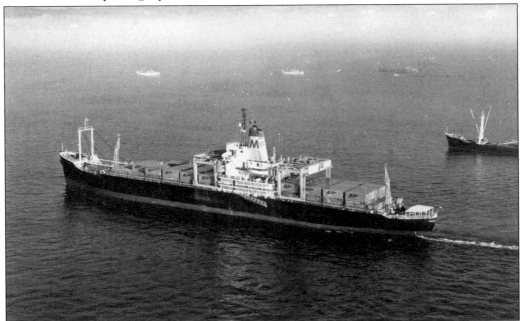

Containers to the Far East, 1967. The Matson Navigation Company's Pacific Coast–Far East container service began with the October 8 sailing of the *Pacific Banker* to Tokyo and Kobe. The ship operated on the route with the *Pacific Trader*. The service was discontinued in 1970 when it proved to be economically impractical. (Courtesy of the Matson Navigation Company.)

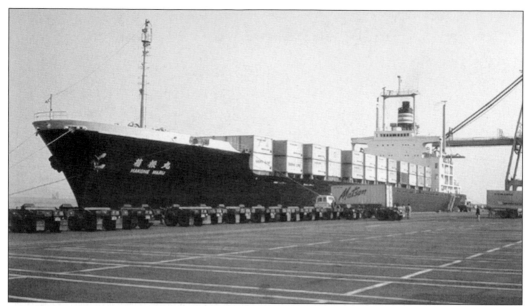

U.S.-JAPAN CONTAINER SERVICE, 1968. History was made at the port in September when the 752-TEU containership *Hakone Maru* called at the Port of Los Angeles, inaugurating the first regular container service between Japan and the United States. The ship was soon joined by two other container ships—the *Haruna Maru* and the *Hakozaki Maru*—on the new service linking the port with Kobe, Nagoya, and Tokyo. (Courtesy of NYK Line.)

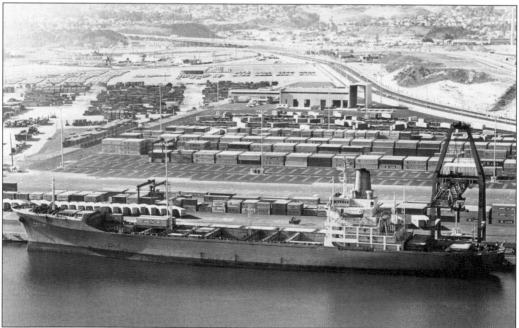

JAPAN CONTAINER TERMINAL, 1969. The 35-acre East-West Container Terminal began operations at Berths 126–131 and served a consortium of four Japanese shipping lines—the Japan Line, Yamashita-Shinnihon Line, Showa Line, and the Mitsui OSK. The facility was later moved to Berths 127–129 and expanded to 42 acres. The terminal was later renamed the Los Angeles Container Terminal with Seatrain Lines as the primary tenant. (Author's collection.)

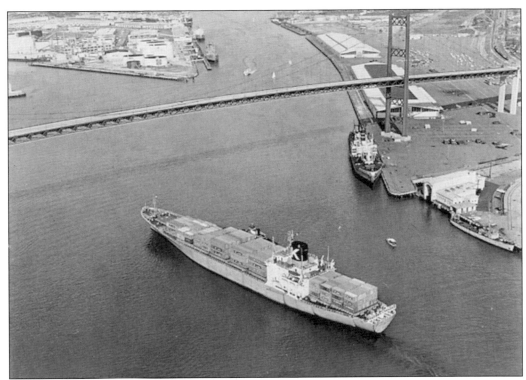

"K" LINE, 1970. An unidentified "K" Line containership passes under the Vincent Thomas Bridge on the way to her berth in the port's West Basin. Kawasaki Kaisen Kaisha, one of Japan's largest shipping lines, began calling at the port before World War I at Berth 230 on Terminal Island. (Author's collection.)

MATSON CONTAINER TERMINAL, 1970. In December, container pioneer Matson Navigation Company completed the development of a 50-acre container facility at Berths 207–209 on Terminal Island near the East Basin. The *Hawaiian Legislator* is seen here being worked by the two container cranes that were moved by barge from Matson's old facility in Wilmington to the new facility. (Author's collection.)

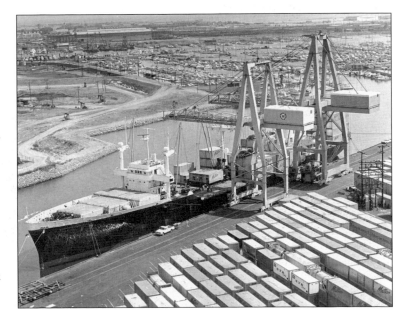

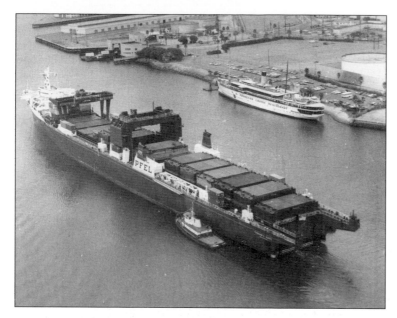

LASH Service, 1971. The Pacific Far East Line's *Thomas E. Cuffe* was the first ship of her type to call at the Port of Los Angeles. LASH technology permitted cargo in 61-foot barges to be moved to and from hard-to-access trade centers at the world's less-developed harbors. The ship is outbound with the Princess Louise Restaurant and the old Terminal Island ferry building to starboard. (Author's collection.)

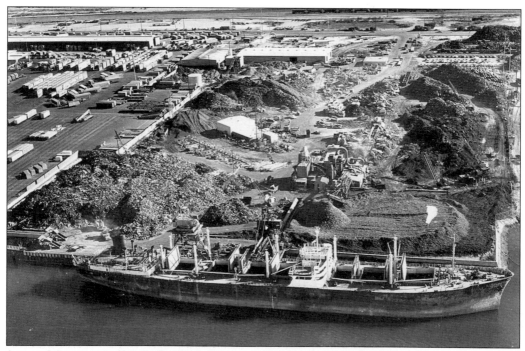

Scrap Metal for Export, 1972. Scrap metal was a major export cargo, with facilities on Terminal Island processing thousands of tons of the material for shipment to the Far East. One of the largest scrap metal processors in the country was the National Metal and Steel Corporation, which acquired the California Shipbuilding Corporation yard a few years after World War II. (Author's collection.)

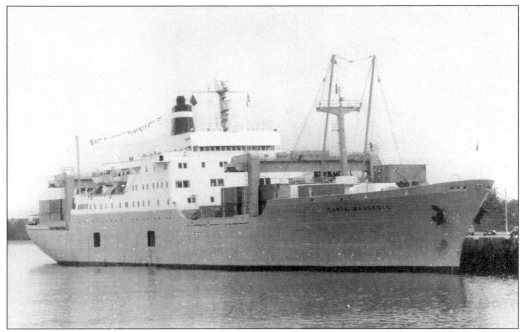

DELTA LINES, 1976. Delta Lines operated four combination passenger-cargo "Santa" ships, including the *Santa Mercedes*, on a route between the U.S. West and Gulf Coasts and Central and South America. The *Santa Mercedes* frequently called at the Port of Los Angeles and, after two decades of service, was converted into a training ship for merchant marine officers. (Author's collection.)

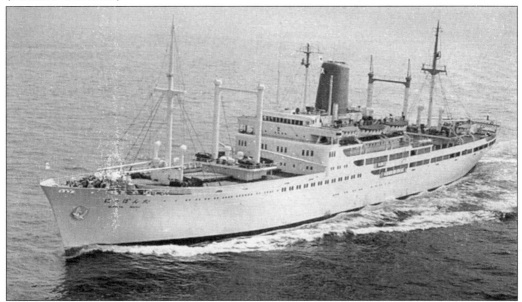

GOODWILL VISIT, 1976. The white-hulled "goodwill ship" *Nippon Maru* visited the Port of Los Angeles in April carrying a delegation of Japanese students and businessmen. The ship was operated by Mitsui OSK Lines and formerly sailed as the passenger liner *Argentina Maru* on a route connecting Japan with the U.S. West Coast and the east coast of South America via the Panama Canal. (Author's collection.)

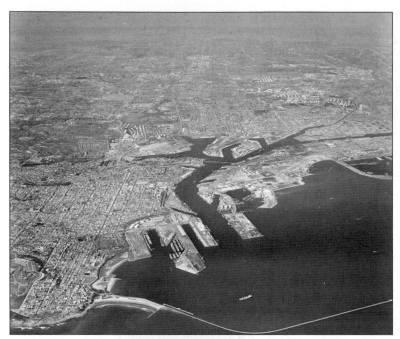

PORT OF LOS ANGELES, 1973. The port sent trade missions to 10 countries, including the first visit to China by a delegation from a U.S. port. Despite a worldwide recession, the port saw significant growth in the 1970s, including an agreement with container giant Evergreen Marine for the development of a container facility on Terminal Island. (Courtesy of the Port of Los Angeles Archive.)

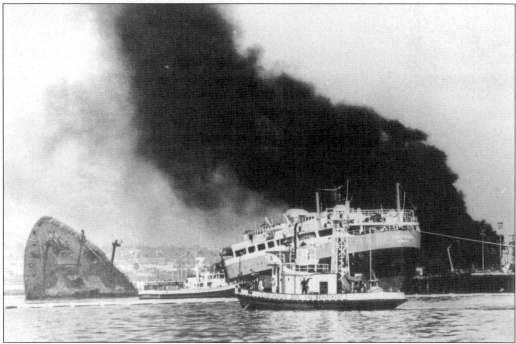

SUPERTANKER BLAST, 1976. Early in the evening of December 17, 1976, the 810-foot supertanker *Sansinena*, empty after unloading a cargo of Indonesian crude at the Union Oil Company's bulk terminal at Berth 46, was blasted in two by an explosion that could be heard 25 miles away in downtown Los Angeles. The exact cause of the explosion was never determined. It was the worst disaster at the port since the steamer *Ada Hancock* blew up in 1863, taking a load of gold to the bottom of the harbor, killing 26 people, and seriously injuring Phineas Banning, his wife, and several other passengers. (Courtesy of the Los Angeles Fire Department Museum.)

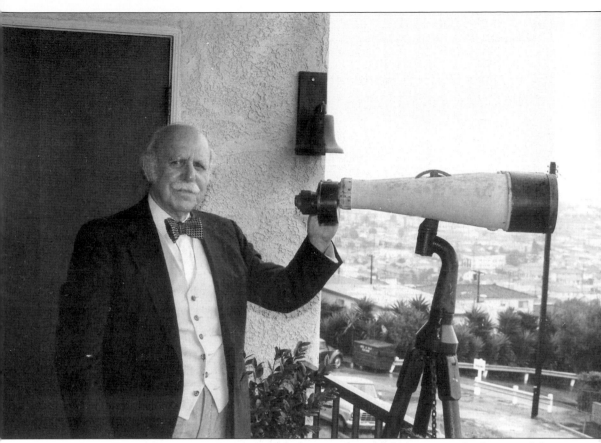

REAR ADM. FRANK HIGBEE, 1981. One of the most endearing characters in the history of the Port of Los Angeles was Frank Higbee. A master mariner who went to sea at the age of 16, Higbee served in the U.S. Navy, U.S. Merchant Marine, and U.S. Coast Guard, from which he retired as a highly decorated flag officer. Higbee had close ties to the Port of Los Angeles as Coast Guard Captain of the Port in the first years of World War II, before taking command in 1945 of a task force of landing ships in the liberation of the Philippines. Following his retirement from the U.S. Coast Guard, he served as port warden in charge of maintaining safety and security at the port's terminals. One of the admiral's favorite pastimes in his later years was using a set of high-powered artillery binoculars set up on the veranda of his apartment on the bluff overlooking the port's Main Channel to watch ships flying the flags of many nations sail in and out of what he called "the best port-of-call in the world." (Author's collection.)

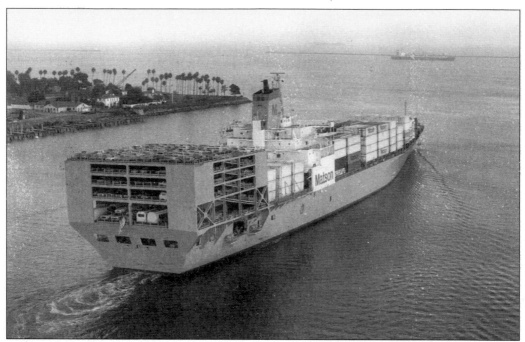

Matsonia, 1987. Launched in 1973, the Matson container ship *Matsonia* was converted into a "roll on–roll off" ship at the Todd Shipyard in San Pedro. The conversion, which cost $44 million, included the lengthening of the ship by 60 feet and the construction of a four-tier, 422-automobile garage on its stern. (Courtesy of the Matson Navigation Company.)

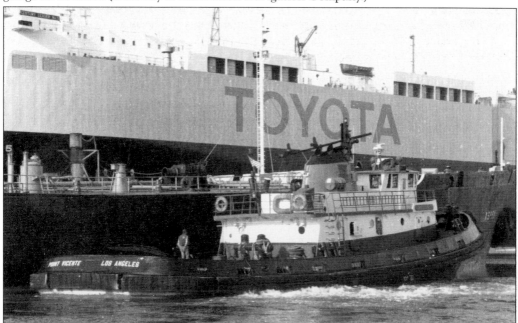

Wilmington Tugboats, 1988. Yellow and brown Wilmington Transportation Company tugs had handled towing and barge-handling duties at the Port of Los Angeles since Phineas Banning incorporated the company in 1884. The company operated at the port until 1989, when its operations were absorbed by the Seattle-based Foss Maritime. (Author's collection.)

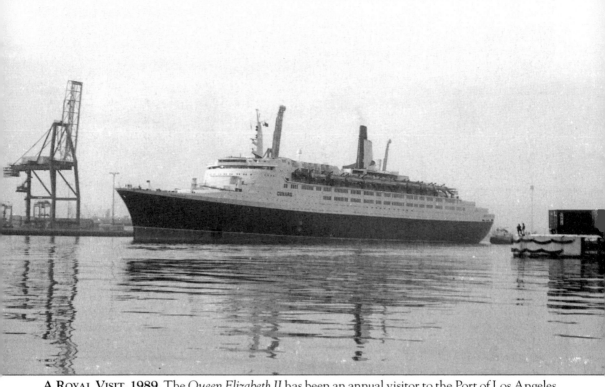

A ROYAL VISIT, 1989. The *Queen Elizabeth II* has been an annual visitor to the Port of Los Angeles since 1969, embarking her passengers at the port's Cruise Terminal. The liner sails under the Cunard house flag and in 2002 became the first ship ever to sail a total of five million miles. Three years later, the *Queen* became the longest-serving ship in the line's history. (Author's collection.)

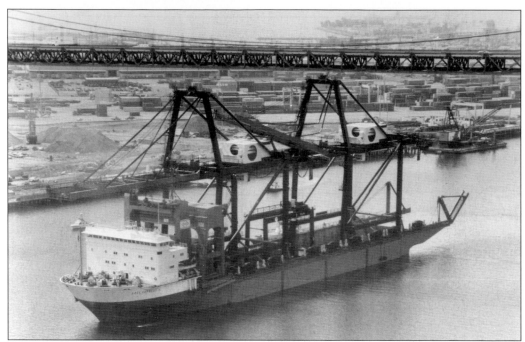

TRAPAC, 1989. With just a few feet to spare, the heavy lift ship *Dock Express II*, pictured here, noses under the Vincent Thomas Bridge with a pair of gantry container cranes manufactured in Japan. The cranes were destined for the Transpacific Container Service Corporation (TRAPAC) container terminal at Berth 136 in the port's Inner Harbor. The multiuser terminal covers 173 acres with 11 container cranes serving five berths and was completed for the company's parent, Mitsui OSK Lines. (Author's collection.)

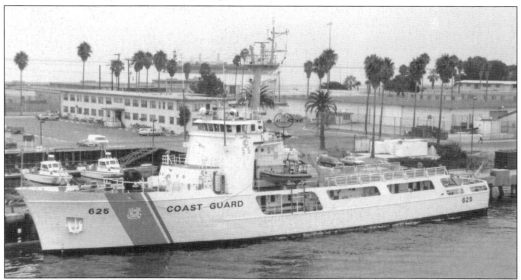

USCGC VENTUROUS, 1990. The U.S. Coast Guard medium-endurance cutter *Venturous* (WMEC 625) was home-ported at the Coast Guard's Port of Los Angeles base for several years. The cutter conducted many search-and-rescue and drug-interdiction missions while based in San Pedro. The base is located at Reservation Point on the port's Main Channel at the southernmost tip of Terminal Island. (Author's collection.)

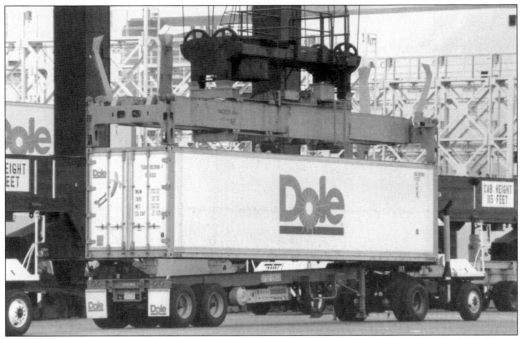

HANDLING CONTAINERS, 1992. A 40-foot container of bananas from Central America is unloaded from a containership onto a waiting chassis. The Port of Los Angeles is the busiest container port in the country, with more than 7.8 million import and export containers—also known as "cans"—moving through the port's eight major container terminals in 2006. (Author's collection.)

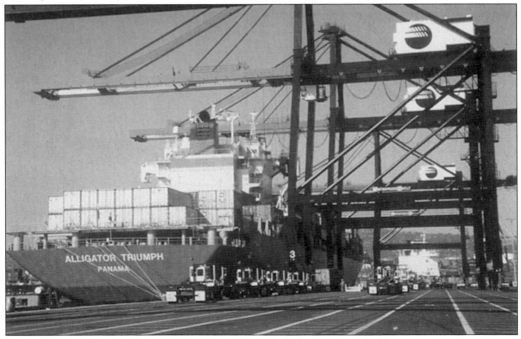

YARD WORK, 1992. Container cranes—each of which can lift 40 tons—can be seen at the TRAPAC Terminal "working" the Mitsui OSK Lines' containership *Alligator Triumph*. (Author's collection.)

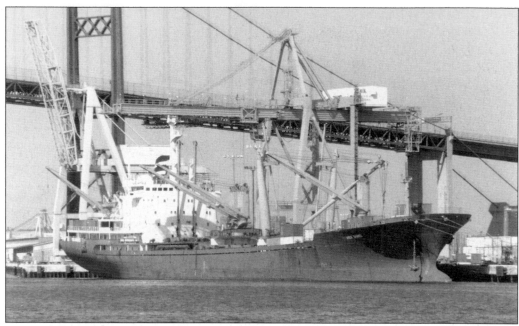

OVERSEAS TERMINAL, 1993. The Overseas Terminal operated in the shadow of the Vincent Thomas Bridge. The facility now operates as the Seaside Container Terminal and covers 205 acres on Terminal Island. (Author's collection.)

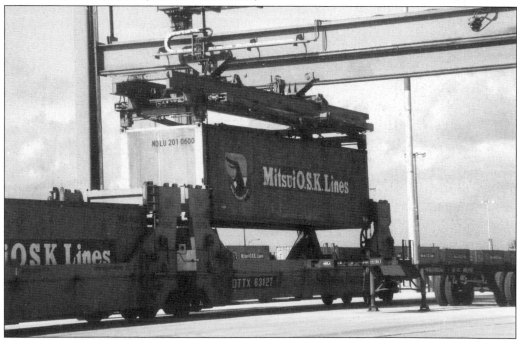

INTERMODAL RAIL, 1995. The port took a leading role in the development of specialized intermodal container facilities that enable the movement of containers between the port's terminals and waiting double-stack trains. The yards have been augmented by the construction of the Alameda Corridor, a below–ground level, multitrack rail line speeding the movement of containers between the port and the intermodal rail terminals near downtown Los Angeles. (Author's collection.)

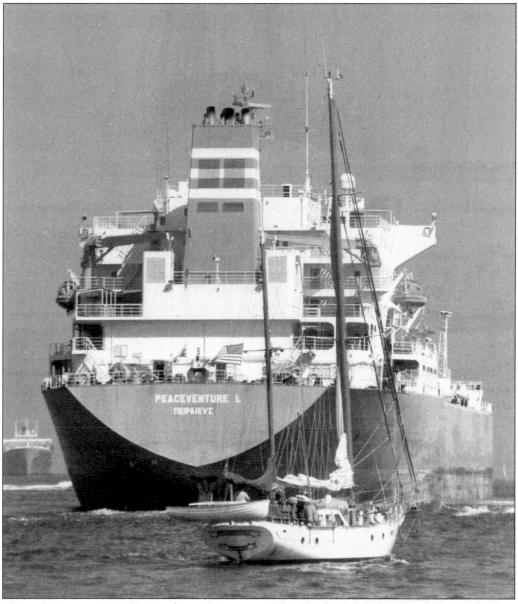

MAIN CHANNEL, 1996. A yacht passes astern of the Greek tanker *Peaceventure L* as the ship heads down the Main Channel toward Angel's Gate and the open sea. The ship is riding high after unloading her cargo of oil at one of the port's petroleum terminals. (Author's collection.)

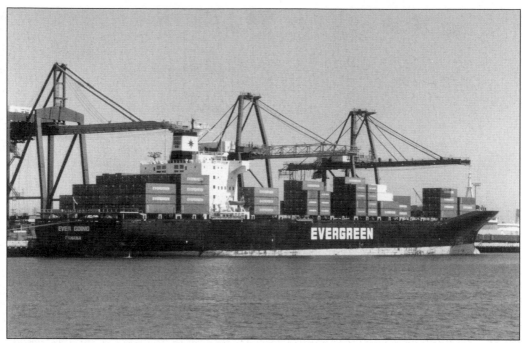

EVERGREEN MARINE, 1997. Taiwan-based Evergreen Marine is one of the largest container carriers in the world and has connected the Far East with the Port of Los Angeles for more than 30 years. The company now operates some of the largest containerships afloat. (Author's collection.)

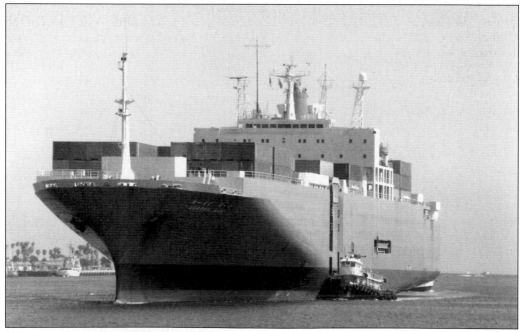

CHANNEL TRAFFIC, 1998. A combination auto/container carrier heads towards its berth at the port's auto terminal at Berths 195–199. The 85-acre auto facility opened in 1969 and has a storage capacity of up to 8,000 vehicles, mostly Nissan, Infiniti, and Nissan diesel cars and trucks. (Author's collection.)

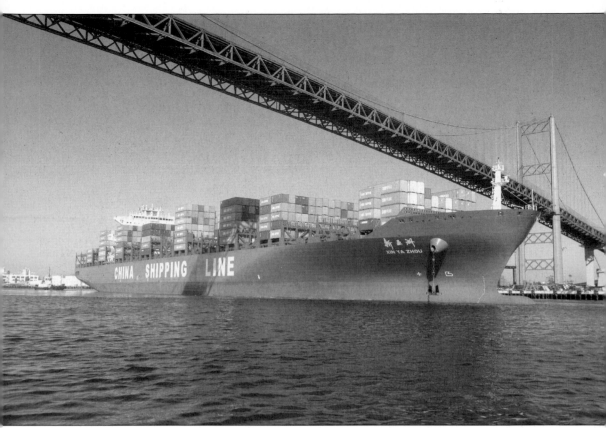

MAIDEN CALL, 2007. The massive container ship *Xin Ya Zhou*, the world's largest alternative maritime power (AMP) ship, passes under the Vincent Thomas Bridge during her September 2007 maiden arrival. The Port of Los Angeles is the only port in the world utilizing environment-friendly AMP technology, which permits visiting container ships to secure their diesel engines and plug into dockside electrical outlets to power their shipboard equipment. (Courtesy of the Port of Los Angeles Archive.)

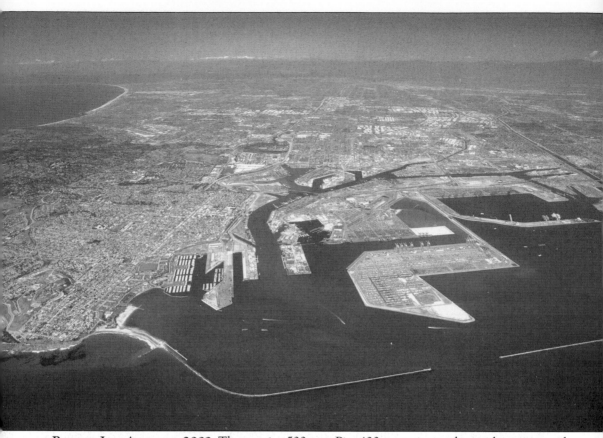

PORT OF LOS ANGELES, 2003. The massive 500-acre Pier 400 extension to the southernmost end of Terminal Island opened after 10 years of dredging and landfill. Maersk SeaLand, the world's largest steamship company, signed on as the terminal's first tenant. The facility (center, right) features 12 on-dock rail tracks and is the largest proprietary container terminal in the world. (Courtesy of the Port of Los Angeles Archive.)

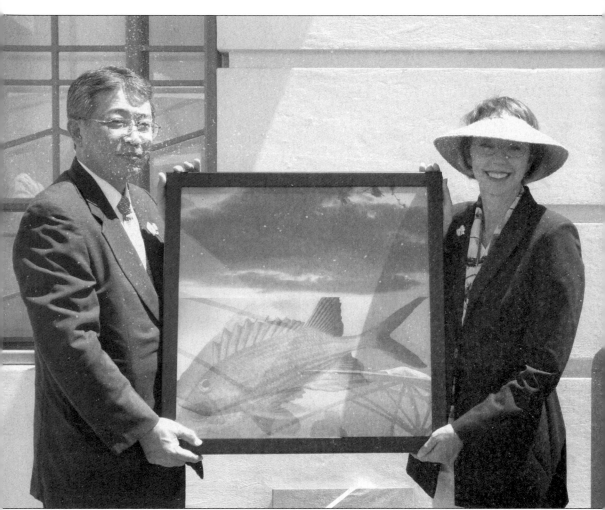

SISTER PORTS, 2007. The Port of Los Angeles and the Port of Nagoya, Japan, both celebrate their 100-year anniversaries in 2007. Dr. Geraldine Knatz, executive director of the Port of Los Angeles, and her counterpart, Takashi Yamada of the Nagoya Port Authority, met in Los Angeles in July to celebrate the occasion. (Courtesy of the Port of Los Angeles Archive.)

BIBLIOGRAPHY

Benson, Howard M. *Steamships and Motorships of the West Coast*. Seattle, WA: Superior Publishing Company, 1968.

Cleland, Robert Glass. *The Cattle on a Thousand Hills*. San Marino, CA: Huntington Library, 1949.

Deverall, William. *Railroad Crossing: Californians and the Railroad 1850–1910*. Berkeley, CA: University of California Press, 1994.

Furita, R. and Y. Hirai. *A Short History of the Japanese Merchant Marine*. Tokyo, Japan: Tokyo News Service Ltd., 1961.

Gibbs, Jim. *Pacific Square Riggers*. New York, NY: Bonanza Books, 1959.

Krieger, Michael. *Where Rails Meet the Sea*. New York, NY: Metro Books, 1998.

Los Angeles Harbor Department. *The Port of Los Angeles: From Wilderness to World Port*. Los Angeles, CA: Los Angeles Harbor Department, 1983.

Marquez, Ernest. *Port Los Angeles*. San Marino, CA: Golden West Books, 1975.

Newell, Gordon and Joe Williamson. *Pacific Lumber Ships*. New York, NY: Bonanza Books, 1960.

O'Flaherty, Joseph S. *Those Powerful Years: The South Coast and Los Angeles 1887–1917*. Los Angeles, CA: The Historical Society of Southern California, 1972.

Quenan, Charles F. *Long Beach and Los Angeles: A Tale of Two Ports*. Northridge, CA: Windsor Publications, 1986.

Spalding, William Andrew. *History and Reminiscences: Los Angeles City and County*. Los Angeles, CA: J. R. Finnell and Sons Publishing Company, 1931.

Stindt, Fred A. *Matson's Century of Ships*. San Francisco, CA: privately published, 1982.

Tate, E. Mowbray. *Transpacific Steam*. Cranbury, NJ: Cornwall Books, 1986.

Vickery, Charles. *Harbor Heritage: Tales of the Harbor Area of Los Angeles, California*. Los Angeles, CA: Authors Book Company, 1979.

INDEX

Al Larson Boat Shop, 63
American President Lines, 87, 88, 101, 102
Angel's Gate, 33
Banning, Phineas, 9, 12–14
California Fish Company, 40
California Shipbuilding Corporation, 78, 79
Cunard Line, 109, 173
Dana, Richard Henry, 11
Deadman's Island, 13, 15
Dollar Steamship Company, 48
E. K. Wood Lumber Company, 25
Evergreen Marine, 122
Hammond Lumber Company, 25, 53
Higbee, Rear Adm. Frank, 170
Huntington, Collis, 16, 17
"K" Line, 67, 111
L.A. City Fireboat No. 2, 50, 53
Los Angeles and San Pedro Railway, 14
Los Angeles Chamber of Commerce, 19, 20
Los Angeles Shipbuilding and Drydock Company, 49, 50
Los Angeles Steamship Company, 35, 46
Los Angeles Terminal Railway, 22
Luckenbach Steamship Company, 70, 71, 92
Matson Navigation Company, 98, 100, 116
McCormick Line, 56, 80
Mitsui Line, 32
Mitsui OSK Line, 118, 119
NYK Line, 30, 61, 96, 97, 110
Oceanic Steamship Company, 98
Pacific Electric Railway, 24
Pacific Far East Line, 88, 112
Pacific Harbor Line, 123
Pacific Steamship Company, 55
Point Fermin Lighthouse, 16, 80
Pope and Talbot, 90
San Pedro, 18, 22

San Pedro Engine Works, 29
Southern California Lumber Company, 30
Southern Pacific Railroad, 18, 19, 24, 31, 45
Southwestern Shipbuilding Company, 39
Standard Oil Company, 38
States Steamship Company, 43
Sunkist Growers, 44, 68
Timms, Augustus, 15
Todd Shipyard, 82, 83
U.S. Borax Company, 57
U.S. Coast Guard, 56, 118
U.S. Shipping Board, 39, 47
USS Constitution, 74, 75
United Fruit Company, 66
Vincent Thomas Bridge, 108
White, Stephen M., 19
Williams Line, 51, 54

ACROSS AMERICA, PEOPLE ARE DISCOVERING SOMETHING WONDERFUL. THEIR HERITAGE.

Arcadia Publishing is the leading local history publisher in the United States. With more than 4,000 titles in print and hundreds of new titles released every year, Arcadia has extensive specialized experience chronicling the history of communities and celebrating America's hidden stories, bringing to life the people, places, and events from the past. To discover the history of other communities across the nation, please visit:

www.arcadiapublishing.com

Customized search tools allow you to find regional history books about the town where you grew up, the cities where your friends and family live, the town where your parents met, or even that retirement spot you've been dreaming about.

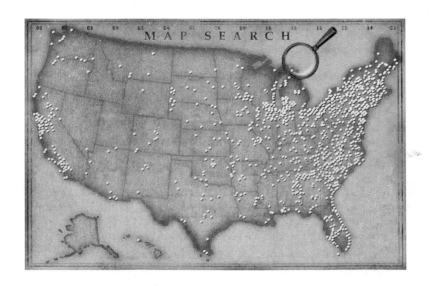